All About Christmas

BY THE SAME AUTHOR

There is a Time to . . .	James Clarke Publishers	1971
Marriage Questions Today	St Andrew Press	1975
Doubts are Not Enough	St Andrew Press	1982
Holy Wit	Gordon Wright Publishing	1986
Laughter Lines	Gordon Wright Publishing	1987
The Master Mind	Handsel Press	1989
More Holy Wit	Gordon Wright Publishing	1990
Keywords of Faith	St Andrew Press	1991

All About Christmas

The Traditions and Meaning
of the Festive Season with a
Good Helping of Humour

from

Rt Rev James A Simpson

(Author of the bestseller *Holy Wit*)

Cartoons by Noel Watson

GORDON WRIGHT PUBLISHING
25 MAYFIELD ROAD, EDINBURGH EH9 2NQ.
SCOTLAND

British Library Cataloguing in Publication Data
A catalogue record for this book is
available from the British Library.

ISBN 0- 903065-81-9

Front cover illustration: Noel Watson.
Cover Design: John Haxby.
Back cover photo: Gordon Wright.

Typeset by Gordon Wright Publishing Ltd., Edinburgh.
Printed and Bound by Butler & Tanner Ltd., Frome, Somerset.

Contents

Preface

I have long wondered whether books should have prefaces at all. They are written last, printed first and read least. The main reason I finally decided to include one, was to indicate that the royalties from this Christmas book will be used to further research into Cystic Fibrosis. It is my sincere hope that the geneticists and doctors working in this field, might soon make it possible for young people like my grand-daughter Sally, to enjoy a better quality of life and many more Christmases. Christmas day is certainly enriched for me by her presence at church and at the Christmas family party.

Acknowledgements

A great deal of work is involved in preparing a manuscript for publication. In this respect I would happily acknowledge my indebtedness to Noel Watson for agreeing to draw the cartoons; my son Allstair for his help with the typing, and to my wife Helen and Dr John Peterson for their helpful suggestions and kindly criticisms.

Diligent effort has been made to locate the copyright-holders of all the material quoted in this book. But in one or two cases this has unfortunately not been possible.

Special acknowledgement and my sincere thanks go to the following: Faber & Faber Ltd; Mirror Group Newspapers; *The Observer*, Toronto; *Life and Work*, Edinburgh; *Presbyterian Survey*; *These Days*, Louisville; The British Library and the Victoria and Albert Museum.

James A Simpson,
Dornoch Cathedral.

To the Peterson family
whose transatlantic friendship
has been such an enriching one.

What is Christmas?

In Britain and many other parts of the world, Christmas is the single most important annual festival. But what essentially is Christmas? That is not an easy question to answer, for Christmas, as we know it today, comprises several overlapping festivals – a commercial festival, a family festival, a festival of friendship and a religious festival.

A Commercial Festival

In Louisa Alcott's classic *Little Women*, Jo grumbles, 'Christmas won't be Christmas without any presents.' The giving and exchanging of presents at Christmas has meant that inevitably Christmas has become a commercial festival. Many stores now depend on Christmas for 50% of their annual sales. As the festive season approaches, manufacturers compete to produce best-sellers. A plastic carrier bag of an Edinburgh store, bore the message 'Christmas is . . .'. The store's name completed the advert. The message was, that in that one store it was possible to buy all the good, tasty, bright, happy Christmas things. At Christmas the cash registers ring more merrily. 'Angels we have heard on high, tell us to go out and buy!'

Christmas comes but once a year but when it comes it lasts four months. Although many feel uneasy about the massive commercial apparatus that has made the carpenter from Nazareth the patron saint of big business, and his birthday often the cause of crippling debt, I would be reluctant to abolish altogether this commercial aspect of Christmas. I enjoy giving presents to loved ones, and surprise gifts to those who mean a great deal to me. But we certainly ought to be on our guard lest our anxiety about there being 'only . . . more shopping days to Christmas' and how we are going to pay the bills, destroys rather than promotes joy and goodwill. 'All the compliments of the Season' can easily become 'all the complaints of the Season'.

*   *   *

Whereas some of us dream of a white Christmas, it leaves most of us in the red.

The Christmas shopper's complaint is one of long standing!

A store detective spoke of 'thirty more shop-lifting days to Christmas.'

Credit cards have three dimensions – height, width and debt.

A new kind of Christmas Club has been proposed – one that would help you save money to pay for last year's gifts.

Christmas is when kids tell Santa Claus what they want and adults later pay for it. Deficits are when adults tell the government what they want and their kids later pay for it.

Anyone who thinks Christmas does not last for six months does not have a charge account.

You must not think of yourself at Christmas. You have to think first and foremost of the economy! The stores are depending on you. If you don't go into debt this year, the shop owners and the nation's economists are going to think you are a rotten person!

The best Christmas gift for a person who has everything is a burglar alarm.

A glamorous girl was bragging about the jewellery her boyfriend had given her for Christmas. 'The trouble with her,' remarked a rival, 'is that she is getting too big for her brooches.'

A Family Festival

Christmas is also a family festival. In the first royal Christmas Day broadcast, King George V described Christmas as the festival of the family. Christmas is not primarily a town or village festival, but a festival celebrated in-doors, in people's homes. Although I feel deeply for those who have unhappy memories of their homes, I am glad that for others the words 'home and family' are still precious, that they conjure up warm memories of give and take, mutual understanding and cheerfulness.

'Home for Christmas.' Many a short story and play have been copyrighted under that title. Home is instinctively where many want to be at Christmas. They travel long distances to be with their family. The greetings are heart-felt. 'Oh lass it is good to see you again.' Home has always been for me the dearest spot on earth. I am glad my parents enjoyed the simple pleasures of the family circle, and that the next three generations of our family still enjoy getting together at Christmas and laughing and reminiscing together.

I grudge not the wealthy whose riches are envied;
I wish them prosperity, favour and more.
But give me the cottage where little feet prattle,
Where love pours the coffee and meets at the door.

We dream of a white Christmas, but the weather does not really matter all that much. Sir Walter Scott wrote:

Heap on more wood! The wind is chill,
But let it whistle as it will —
We'll keep our Christmas merry still.

* * *

Keeping peace in the family at Christmas requires patience, love, understanding and at least two T.V. sets.

Spending Christmas in America, Sir David Frost was entering his hotel when he almost collided with a man burdened with bottles of whisky and wine. When Frost observed that Christmas is hard work, the American replied, 'Yep, we'd never do it if it wasn't for the kids.'

American parents gave their son a car as a Christmas present. On the windscreen was a card signed, 'With love, Mama and Pauper.'

Happy laughter in the home will keep more kids off the street than the strictest curfew.

One rainy day just before Christmas, a Mrs Mann heard a mother say to her eight-year-old, outside a department store: 'Button up tight and stand here until I come back. I want to know if your coat is still waterproof.' As they filed through the doors Mrs Mann asked her if she always tested her son's coats that way. 'No,' she replied, 'but how else can I go in and buy him his Christmas present.'

When the mid-wife at the hospital informed little Sam he had a new baby brother for Christmas, Sam said, 'Could I be the first to tell Mummy?'

The hardest meal for mother to get at Christmas is breakfast in bed.

A Festival of Friendship

Many at Christmas are more thoughtful of those who have little or nothing to call their own, and those who sit by forgotten firesides. It is a time when many are moved to give generously to charities and good causes, and to send surprise cards to people who live alone. As we grow older we have friends from childhood, friends from schooldays, friends from the various places in which we have lived and worked. Christmas cards have helped keep many of these friendships alive. They help recall voices and faces from the past.

It has been suggested that the main reason why we should post Christmas cards early is to make it possible for the receiver to reciprocate! But surely something has gone far wrong when the sending of cards becomes little more than the 'trading' of cards, when offence is caused, and relationships strained, because no card was received for one sent.

*   *   *

A film star was telling another that she bought all her Christmas cards and presents in October. 'But how do you know in October who your friends are going to be in December?'

When Mike was asked why he had not spoken to Patrick after the Midnight Mass, he explained that it was not that they had quarrelled. In fact they were the best of friends. 'Pat and I are that devoted to wan another that we can't bear the idea of a quarrel; and as we are both moighty quick-tempered, we've resolved not to spake to wan another at all, for fear we break the friendship.'

One year as Christmas approached, Andrew Carnegie, the multi-millionaire, wagered his sister-in-law that he could get a letter from her uncommunicative son. He wrote his nephew a chatty note ending with the message that he was enclosing A CHEQUE. By *not* enclosing the cheque he won an immediate response – and his bet.

After much urging from her mother a little girl wrote the following thank you note: 'Thank you for your nice Christmas present. I always wanted a pin cushion although not very much.'

A Religious Festival

Christmas without its spiritual richness can easily become little more than an exercise in overspending and overeating, in wrapping up presents and untangling Christmas tree lights.

A school-teacher in England was supervising the construction of a manger scene in a corner of the classroom. The barn had been set up the floor covered with real straw – then the clay figures of Mary and Joseph, the shepherds and the wise men, and the animals. All were placed to face a small crib in which lay a tiny doll representing the baby Jesus. One little boy in the classroom couldn't tear himself away from the Nativity scene. He kept returning to it. He stood there completely engrossed with a puzzled expression on his face. Eventually the teacher went up to him and asked what was bothering him. With his eyes still glued to the manger scene, the boy said, 'What I'd like to know is, where does God fit in?'

In this book I have no intention of playing the peevish spoil-sport, complaining that the church's festival has been stolen by the secular world. Instead I want to look at how the church at various times borrowed or hi-jacked bright and interesting rituals and customs from the winter festivals of the Romans, the Druids and the Norsemen, and then remodelled them, giving them at the same time new meaning. As well as looking at many of the happy celebrations associated with a late 20th century Christmas, such as Christmas trees and pear trees, holly and ivy, carols and crackers, Santa and reindeer, I want also to look at where God fits in to Christmas.

*   *   *

An old man in Fife told a friend he was a regular church attender – every Christmas Eve.

13

A wayside pulpit notice read, 'Heaven knows when you were here last.'

An American woman came to see her minister with what she described as a difficult problem. She explained that she was Chairperson of a community Christmas Tree Celebration, and was having great difficulty selecting the songs for the occasion. 'The Christmas Carols are all so distressingly theological.' As graciously as he could the minister pointed out that Christmas was a rather theological affair!

One Christmas the minister concluded his prayer with the words, 'O Lord give us this Christmas pure hearts, peaceful hearts, *sweet hearts*.' I could imagine teenage girls in the congregation gladly responding 'Ah-men!'

James Dent tells of two young girls who came across a painting of Mary and the baby Jesus. 'See there,' said the older girl, 'that's Jesus and that's his mother.' 'Where's his father?' asked the younger girl. Her older sister thought for a moment and then explained, 'Oh he's taking the picture.'

An American story illustrates how we sometimes unwittingly juxtapose two quite contradictory statements. An oil-worker who attended church one Christmas Eve, placed by mistake in the collection plate the fifty dollar bill he had in his pocket instead of the five dollar one. After the service he asked the usher if he might switch them. Not knowing the man, the usher expressed regret that he could not really do this. The kindly roughneck accepted this, saying, 'Oh well, it's for the Lord, so to hell with it.'

And Jesus said unto them, 'Who do you say that I am?' And they replied, 'You are the eschatological manifestation of the ground of our being. . . .' And Jesus said, 'What?'

Christmas - December 25th?

We do not know the month, let alone the exact date of the birth of Jesus. In fact the more literally you take the biblical records, the less likely a mid-winter nativity becomes. Shepherds spending the night in the fields suggests spring rather than winter. The first historical record of Jesus' birthday being celebrated in December, comes from the early 4th century. It was then that Julius I, the Bishop of Rome, officially established this festival of the church.

One possibility for the choice of December 25th, has been the suggestion that some early church thinkers felt that Jesus' life must have exhibited perfect chronology, that he must have lived an exact number of years. Now the preferred date for his crucifixion was March 25th. This they believed must also have been the date of his conception. Add nine months and you get December 25th.

But far more likely was the fact that in the year 274 A.D. the Roman Emperor Aurelian gave official recognition to the festival of the Persian god Mithra, the Invincible Sun-God. This festival took place on December 25th. For some time previously Roman soldiers and others had on that date celebrated the sun recovering its vigour. About that time of year also, Romans had for centuries taken part in a festival honouring Saturn, the god of agriculture and the legendary ruler of Rome in a former golden age. This festival which was called the Saturnalia was a time for giving presents. It was also a time of peace and goodwill, a time when people forgave their enemies, when master and slaves bathed together.

Christmas is the classic example of the Christian church coming to terms with pagan customs and rites. As Christianity gained the ascendancy over rival cults, they superimposed a Christian festival upon a pagan mid-winter holiday. Christians chose the December date to celebrate the birth of Jesus, the Sun of Righteousness.

✦   ✦   ✦

Christmas is not a date. It's a state of mind.

God so loved the world . . . that he did not send a committee.

Hearing a businessman say, 'This could be the greatest Christmas ever.' a colleague commented, 'I always thought the first one was.'

A small boy was overheard saying to his new baby sister, whom he had been told was 'a gift from God'. 'Quick, before you forget, what does God look like?'

On a billboard entitled 'Christmas Holiday *Services*', British Rail intimated that there would be no trains on Christmas Day or Boxing Day.

Lloyd Douglas told a story about a mean old Scrooge who broke a needle in his foot. Part of the needle was immediately recovered, but the other half could not be found. Despite the doctor's assurances, the old man became convinced that the missing piece was in his bloodstream, heading towards his heart. Under threat of death, he reformed his ways. Contrary to his imaginings he did not die. That year on Christmas day his wife presented him with the other half of the needle. She had found it shortly after the accident, but her husband's character had been so transformed, that she had refrained from telling him.

An eight-year-old wrote: 'I like Christmas because it is then we go into the attic and get all kinds of stuff and light up the world.'

Popularising Christmas

Much of the Christmas ritual which we today take for granted is in fact relatively recent. At the beginning of Queen Victoria's reign in 1837, British children did not hang their stockings by the fireplace on Christmas Eve; nobody had heard of Santa Claus; Christmas crackers did not exist; few people ate turkey on Christmas day. It was not common then to give presents at Christmas and the decorated and brightly lit Christmas tree was hardly known outside the Royal Court. In fact in 1837, and for a long time afterwards in England, and for even longer in Scotland, Christmas day was not observed as a holiday. It was not a day of feasting or any kind of social ritual. It was not until the late 19th century in England that the modern Christmas ritual began to take shape, and even then it was, to begin with, a festival confined mostly to the middle and upper classes.

In the 17th century the English Puritans strongly objected to all the 'drinking and feasting' that went on at Christmas. The Puritan Parliament passed a law in 1644 making December 25th a fast day rather than a feast day, a day when the nation would repent of its sins. They ordered troops to go round London ensuring that no Christmas dinners were being cooked. Inspectors were appointed to wander the streets sniffing out bakers indulging in the illicit practice of producing mince pies. The House of Commons sat on Christmas day and shops stayed open by order.

In tracing the history of Christmas we find that Dickens had a great deal to do with the reappearance of Christmas as a popular festival in England, just as Washington Irving had much to do with its development in the U.S.A. Dickens was responsible for many of the characteristics that we associate with Christmas today. His *Christmas Carol* has been described as 'the second greatest Christmas story ever told'. Its characters are unforgettable – Tiny Tim with his crutches, the miser Scrooge who finally learns the true spirit of Christmas, and Bob Cratchit drinking Christmas cheer despite awful poverty. It was this book, and Dickens' vivid description of Christmas at Dingley Dell in the *Pickwick Papers*, that popularised many of the aspects of Christmas that we know today – family gatherings, seasonal drinks, magnificent meals, plum pudding, and games enjoyed in front of a blazing Yule log. People began to warm to the idea of Christmas. 'Merry Christmas' became a common greeting.

The Christmas that developed had a spiritual significance, but it was less a Christian spirituality than one which drew heavily upon the warm humanitarianism epitomised by Charles Dickens. It saluted and celebrated the nuclear family childhood and the extended family.

The festival as it developed in England in the 19th century borrowed much of its imagery and ritual from Germany where the Christmas festival had long been highly valued.

In Scotland the resistance to the Christmas festival lasted longer than in England. Many in Scotland regarded it as a pagan festival. An Edinburgh man tells how early this century when he asked his grandmother, 'Why do we not celebrate Christmas in Scotland?', her answer was, 'We're no heathens laddie.' The Scottish reformers had taught that the celebration of Christmas had 'neither commandment nor assurance in God's Scriptures.' They pointed out that the nativity festival had not been part of the life of the early Church.

Another reason for the resistance to Christmas north of the Border was that Scotland had its own rival New Year celebrations. On Hogmanay night children hung up their stockings to be filled. The ritual of 'first-footing' armed with a lump of coal and a cake was a deeply rooted custom. A Perthshire man Henry Kinnaird described Christmas in the years after the First World War, 'We did not have a holiday on Christmas Day. We went to school. It felt quite normal because work was going on in the farms and villages; shops were working and so were the mills. There was a soup kitchen which was run during the winter, and as a special treat for Christmas, you got pieces of chicken in the soup which went down well.'

By this time there was a further reason for the resistance to Christmas. Presbyterian Scotland regarded the recently revived festival south of the Border as 'English'. It was for Episcopalians and Roman Catholics who knew no better!

Despite all this prejudice against Christmas, the festival did however gradually begin to creep back into Scotland. Two world wars, the shrinking of the earth through speedier means of transport and communication, the advent of radio and then television, had brought growing awareness of the world-wide church and its traditions. Christmas was gradually reborn. But it was not until 1958 that Christmas became a public holiday in Scotland.

St Nicholas

St Nicholas was a real person though much of what is known about him is legendary. Paintings by the world's masters immortalise many of the miracles attributed to him. It is so difficult to separate fact from fiction that a recent Pope finally decided to remove Nicholas' name and feast day from the Roman Catholic Calendar of saints. Yet in the Russian Orthodox Church he still ranks in holiness next to Mary. Nicholas was probably born late in the third century in Turkey. He became a Christian and eventually Bishop of Myra. With other Christians he was imprisoned by the Roman Emperor Diocletian, but released around 306 AD. But even these dates are uncertain. What we do know for certain is that he had a remarkably kind and generous nature.

His link with Christmas rests mainly on a story which tells how Bishop Nicholas came to the rescue of a needy neighbour who had three daughters of marriageable age. Apparently it was the tradition in Turkey for such girls to present their future husbands with a dowry. St Nicholas had heard that the girls' father was so poor he could not afford to give his daughters dowries. The girls were naturally upset being thus prevented from marrying. So on three successive nights he climbed on to the roof of their house and dropped purses containing gold coins down the chimney. The purses landed in the stockings which the girls had washed and hung by the fire to dry. When the father ultimately found out who the benefactor was, Nicholas pledged him to silence. It was this story that evoked many Christmas practices such as hanging stockings by the chimney, and giving presents anonymously.

The St Nicholas legends and traditions were introduced to North America by the early Dutch settlers. Wood-cuts from around 1810 show St Nicholas tall and dignified in bishop's attire, drawn through the sky by horses. The American writer Washington Irving, by sharing with his readers descriptions of Dutch Christmas customs, did much to establish the American Christmas cult. Irving was in fact the first to describe St Nick's famous gesture, 'laying a finger beside his nose.'

Santa Claus

It is hard for us today to imagine Christmas without Father Christmas or Santa Claus – now interchangeable names for the same imaginary being. In the days leading up to Christmas he twinkles at us from countless posters, shop windows and Christmas cards. He appears at parties, and can be visited in most big stores. But Santa as we know him today did not exist until the 1860s. His most famous ancestors were *Christkindl*, the Swiss tradition of the Christ child drawn by tiny deer on a sleigh ride, and St Nicholas.

The modern Santa was the creation of a Bavarian, Thomas Nast who drew illustrations for *Harper's Weekly*. In 1863 Nast began a series of drawings of Santa. His initial drawings reflected current ideas of St Nicholas, with a few embellishments. In his later Christmas drawings however, the Santa Claus legend is considerably embellished: the North Pole workshop, the elves, the spyglass to enable Santa to find out who is naughty and who is nice. . . . Although Santa originally appeared in these drawings as a gnome, by 1880 he had matured into the full-size, red-robed, lovable grandfather figure we know so well today.

The toys may look different, but the Santa that Thomas Nast drew in 1879 for *Harper's Weekly* is remarkably like the modern Santa Claus.

The popularity of Clement Moore's poem about 'St Nick', "'Twas the night before Christmas', published in 1823, greatly influenced Nast's early illustrations. 'His cheeks were like roses, his nose like a cherry.' Although this poem did not mention Santa, it did much to mould children's thoughts about the jovial old man who comes and fills children's stockings at Christmas.

* * *

Christmas is the time for wishpering in Santa's ear.

From a small child's school essay: 'Santa has a white wool face with rouge cheeks and false teeth and wears a red bonnet. He holds your hand and says, "Howjer do" and says, "I'll give you anything you want if you're good." He lives with God except if it snows. Then he stays at Harrods.'

Victor Borge said: 'Santa Claus has the right idea. Visit people once a year.'

Young girl: 'Do you think Father Christmas will be able to find us in our new house?' Brother: 'Of course he will. God knows where we are all the time and he will tell Jesus and Jesus will tell Father Christmas.'

'Santa is even-tempered. Santa does not hit children who kick him. Santa uses the term 'folks' rather than Mummy and Daddy because of all the broken homes. Santa does not have a three-martini lunch. Santa wears a good deodorant.' (Instructions given to Employees of Western Temporary Services, the world's largest suppliers of Santa Clauses.)

A little girl told her teacher: 'Santa didn't bring me what I wanted. Daddy says he must have bumped his head as he was coming down the chimney and got all confused.' 'What did you want?' asked the teacher. 'A baby.' she replied.

'I have a great deal of sympathy for Santa's long-suffering wife, Mrs Claus. After all, there can't be too many other wives willing to put up with a husband who, year after year, keeps reindeer as domestic pets by his fireside chair – who expects her to run round town in a sledge rather than a Rover, and who stays out all night on Christmas Eve, eventually coming home sloshed on other women's sherry with the ridiculous excuse of having spent the night shinning up and down other people's chimneys to fill stockings with things to give to children who (he insists) are definitely not his own.'
Miranda Grassie, *Sunday Times,* 23 December 1984.

A friend of the Rev James Currie took his little niece from Cardiff into an Edinburgh store to see Santa. Santa placed the little girl on his knee and said, 'Ho, Ho, Ho. What a bonny Scots lassie we have here.' 'But I'm not Scottish, I'm Welsh,' said Megan. 'Oh you *are* from Wales' said Santa. 'I did my national service there.' I don't suppose in these days of supersonic reindeer, Lapland is that far away from Leekland, but that encounter with Santa certainly gave that uncle plenty of explaining to do.

A father was chatting to his young son about Christmas: 'Santa brings toys to good little boys. Do you know what he brings if you're bad?' 'Clothes, I suppose.'

'Santa Claus's Rebuke' by Thomas Nast. This drawing is subtitled, 'I'll never do it again', yet the reader is led to believe that Nast's jolly elf will give a present after delivering his rebuke.

A Radio Scotland newscaster tells how her three-year-old was asked early one December, 'What are you going to do at Christmas?' The reply was not what the inquirer or his mother expected. 'Behave' he said.

A Mrs Tranter tells how her friend's five-year-old son John attended the local church school. When the school chaplain visited the classroom he was always dressed in 'mufti'. The children knew him simply as Mr Williams. Before Christmas there was the usual school party. When he came home, John's mother asked him if Santa had been there. 'It wasn't really Santa,' said John. 'It was Mr Williams pretending to be Santa.' A few weeks later when John attended a church service, his mother asked if he had seen anyone he knew. 'Yes,' John replied, 'I saw Mr Williams, and guess what – he's pretending to be a minister now!'

Christmas Carols

The tradition of carol singing round the streets is much older than Christmas itself. In the ancient pagan winter solstice festivals, 'carols' were sung to accompany the frenzied dancing in rings. The word carol means 'ring dance'. The Christian church, having decided to hold the festival of the nativity at the same time as these pagan Roman festivals, not surprisingly hi-jacked the carol. Poets and composers were encouraged to write Christmas music, but their efforts were for the most part formal and lacking in real joy. This concerned St Francis. He encouraged his fellow monks to write Christmas words to popular songs and to sing them in the village streets. The mediaeval carol was an attempt to introduce a more joyful note into worship.

But the strong reaction of Cromwell's Long Parliament in the 17th century to the gaiety of Christmas and carols, resulted in a steady decline of interest in carol singing. Davies Gilbert the M.P. for Bodmin, who published the first modern collection of traditional carols in 1822, spoke of them as unfortunately being a thing of the past. These carols had for the most part been handed down by oral tradition. The singing of carols in church was not revived until the 19th century, when Dickens' novels made Christmas much more popular.

In 1918 a festival of nine lessons and carols was started in Kings College Cambridge, beginning with the processional hymn, 'Once in Royal David's City'. It has continued ever since, being seen regularly by millions of television viewers at Christmas.
Since the First World War, carols have become more and more popular.

More people can sing 'Silent Night' than can recite the 23rd Psalm, and more folks learn the nature of the gifts which were brought to the baby Jesus from the carol 'We Three Kings', than from reading the Bible.

The carols remind us not only of the Bethlehem story but of many of the traditions and beliefs that grew up round that story. For example the line 'ox and ass before him bow' recalls the old belief that on Christmas Eve cattle and sheep turn to the East and kneel in homage.

* * *

Lady Marion Fraser was teaching piano to a seven-year-old. As Christmas approached she asked him which carol he would like to learn to play. 'The one about the three wee kings.'

A woman who had failed her driving test five times finally passed the week before Christmas, She understandably phoned her husband to tell him the good news. That night when he returned home, he came into the kitchen singing 'Noel, Noel.'

A choirmaster was overheard saying to a choir-boy, 'No no Carruthers, 'Hark the Herald Angels Sing' was written by Wesley, not Presley.'

Herb Caen in *One Man's San Francisco* tells how one Christmas, a resident of the elegant community of Hillsborough, California, accompanied by his wife and children, set out to sing carols for the neighbours. As they were tuning up outside the first house, the woman came to the door looking distraught. 'Look, I'm just too busy. The plumbing is on the blink. I can't get anybody to fix it, and there's a mob coming for dinner. If you really feel like carol singing, come back at nine o' clock.' 'Yes ma'am,' replied Bing Crosby respectfully as he herded his troupe elsewhere.

Robert Morley writes: 'Before Christmas the anticipation of, and the actual arrival of carol singers on the doorstep is the first anxiety of Christmas for most people. The very notion of a band of strangers or, what is worse, neighbours pretending to be wandering minstrels and beseeching alms after completing a ragged verse or two of 'Good King Wenceslas', is one no householder can take in his stride. Dare one cut them off almost at the start by flinging open the front door and calling out, 'Happy Christmas. Anyone for Coke or sherry?'

One Christmas a church bulletin gave exciting ecclesiastical authority to 'Sing choir of angels, sin in exultation.'

A radio announcer, previewing forthcoming live broadcasts told how over the Christmas period there would be live broadcasts of two major choral works, Handel's 'Messiah' and Haydn's 'Cremation'.

A White Christmas

It was Dickens who first propagated the myth that a really good Christmas should be white. Irving Berlin later developed this idea in what was to become one of the most popular songs of all time. 'I'm dreaming of a white Christmas . . . where the tree-tops glisten and children listen to hear sleigh bells in the snow.' It has been pointed out that Irving Berlin wrote it sunning himself under a palm tree. Berlin got his year round tan dreaming about white Christmases, but staying well away from them.
Another enduring contribution to 20th century Christmas legend has been

the song composed by Johnny Marks in 1949 about Rudolph! It is a story not about an under-dog, but an 'under-deer' who makes good. Though Rudolph was the butt of jokes among his reindeer companions because of his shiny red nose, he finally triumphs one Christmas Eve when the sky is overcast and the shining nose enables Santa and his reindeer team to find their way and deliver presents.

Queen Victoria's Christmas tree, 1848. Engraving from *Illustrated London News*.

The Christmas Tree

It is difficult to be certain when the fir tree first came to be linked with the celebration of the birth of Christ. According to a legend which comes down to us from the early days of Christianity in Britain, a monk named Saint Wilfred felled a great oak tree, which in the Druid religion was an object of worship. As it fell to the earth, the oak tree split. Later from its centre there grew up a young fir tree. This tree was dedicated to the Christ-child. 'Its wood,' the saint said, 'is the wood of peace for your houses are built of fir. It is the sign of endless life for its leaves are evergreen.' A similar story is told about St Boniface in Germany.

The Christmas tree was an integral part of the German celebration of Christmas long before it became part of our Christmas festivities. It was not in fact until about 1841 that Prince Albert, who had brought with him from Germany a wealth of German Christmas lore, arranged for a Christmas tree to be installed in Windsor Castle for Queen Victoria. It was 1912 before Madison Square in New York had its first Christmas tree, and many years later before a similar tree appeared in the square of any British town. Yet today, topped with either a star or an angel, and glittering with 'fairy' lights and decorations, Christmas trees stand proudly in most churches, town squares and millions of homes throughout Britain.

The fascination with 'lit' Christmas trees reaches back to the pagan festivals of Saturnalia and Yuletide in which there had been the ritual of fire, and in which evergreens had acted as a kind of fertility rite to ensure the coming of spring. In late 19th century Britain, candles in special holders were perched on the branches of the Christmas tree. These candles were lit on Christmas Day. It was a spectacular sight, but very dangerous. Numerous tragedies resulted from the branches bursting into flames, or people's clothes catching fire as they brushed past the tree. The fire risk was considerably minimised when in the 1890s the discovery of electricity made possible powered 'fairy lights'. The early Christmas trees were also often decked out with Union Jacks and the flags of the Empire, for Christmas was then closely bound up with nationalism and imperialism.

*   *   *

As Christmas approaches, foresters go on a 'chopping' spree.

An American family lived for many years in a remote part of India. The youngest was three the last year they were in India, and four the first Christmas they returned to the United States. Her brothers, a few years older had vague recollections of snow and fir trees. They had missed these treats while they were abroad. Their parents had not been able to find in India anything more festive than a white artificial tree for the presents to go under. When the father brought home a fragrant green spruce for their first American Christmas, the youngest child was inconsolable. 'That's not a Christmas tree,' she sobbed, 'I want a real Christmas tree like the white one we had last year.'

A lady once wrote to the *Milwaukee Journal* asking, 'Where can I buy aluminium Christmas tree needles to spread on the carpet under my aluminium Christmas tree. I want it to look natural.'

Another problem with the new fangled tree is that they don't ever have 'a bad side'. Each year my wife is heard to say, 'Turn it just a little . . . a bit more . . . so that the bad side is to the wall.'

The price of a Christmas tree being dependent on its height, the one benefit in the increase of the price of Christmas trees, is that it is now easier, when decorating the tree, to reach the top!

The Christmas Stocking

Today the Christmas stocking is an elaborate and often costly affair. But in many homes in Scotland earlier this century, the Christmas stocking was often three-quarters-filled with old newspapers. Above the newspaper, parents then put an orange, a new penny, a piece of shortbread and a few sweets. Changes for the better in people's financial circumstances, later made possible the filling of the Christmas stocking with goodies from the toe upwards.

Changes in fashion have however recently created problems for the magical

Christmas stocking. Long socks are less common today than fifty years ago. Whereas I wore short trousers and long socks until I was in my teens, today from an early age boys wear long trousers and short socks, and girls wear warm tights. The drawback of using tights for a Christmas stocking is that both legs would have to be filled with goodies!

Some people have strong convictions about the Christmas stocking. It not only has to be the right size, it has to have the right feel in the dark, the right taste, and of course a Christmassy smell. This means that a tangerine or an apple, talc and perfume are basic ingredients. So too are chocolate coins, or a macaroon bar or a sugar mouse. My wife is convinced that without these basic ingredients, you have not got an authentic Christmas stocking. When our children were young the stocking also had to include a small torch to enable them to examine the stocking contents in the dark. Another essential ingredient was the toothbrush. Just as August 1st is for many the day for purchasing a new car, so in our family 25 December was the occasion for getting a new toothbrush.

No electric train set or doll can quite match the magic of a Christmas stocking that has been filled with thought and care. A close friend starts planning 'surprises' for his wife's stocking early in November. (Unlike me he does not enlist the help of a married daughter.) The amount of thought he puts into that stocking is an expression of his love for his wife.

*　　*　　*

Love is what makes the Christmas stocking such a magical cave of delights. Without love all you have is a cylindrical parcel.

Many a parent sighs for the good old days when a stocking could actually hold what a child wanted for Christmas.

Thank you Mum for not listening to me when I sang 'All I want for Christmas is my two front teeth.' Thank you Dad for not putting coal in my stocking despite your warnings that I might deserve it.

G K Chesterton once commented on the fact that many thank God for the presents in their stockings, but few give Him thanks that they have legs in their stockings.

A broadcaster in Los Angeles employed a personal gift consultant to choose and buy Christmas gifts for his wife's stocking.

'Have you any that would teach my husband how to finish what he starts?'

Abolishing Christmas

A member of our youth group had been asked to propose the motion that 'Christmas has been so commercialised and secularised that it is fit only to be abolished.' I did what I could to help her present a strong case. I pointed out:

— that Christmas seems to be steadily advancing backwards. It is now no longer one special day, but a prolonged business festival. Christmas lights appear in the streets more than two months before 25 December, not to mention Christmas clubs which flourish mid-summer. As Christmas approaches shoppers become progressively more aggressive, and shop-keepers more irritable. Anyone caught in the last minute Christmas rush soon learns that there is a great deal of the beast left in most of us. Anyone found trying to jump the queue is liable to be savagely attacked, physically or verbally.

— that the little obese robin which stares at us from so many Christmas cards is a pretty accurate symbol of what Christmas has become for many – a time when we gorge ourselves on food and drink and even larger dollops of sentiment.

— the considerable drain which the build-up to Christmas has on people's emotions and finances, and the strain it can put on marriages.

— that it is hypocrisy to call an annual orgy of self-indulgence and a gigantic spending spree, which many cannot afford, after one who said, 'Beware, be on your guard against greed of every kind.'

— that the well known Christmas song could be rewritten, 'on the 12th day of Christmas my true love sent to me, five anadins, one massive overdraft and the last of the turkey.'

— that the holiday spirit sometimes eclipses the spirit of the holy-day.

Together we made out a pretty good case for abolishing Christmas. The problem was that neither of us really believed in what we were advocating. I long to reform Christmas, but not to abolish it. For me part of the miracle of Christmas is that despite all our efforts, we have not succeeded in completely ruining the festival.

Despite the excessive commercialism, I still believe in Christmas. I enjoy the smells of Christmas, the piny-sprucy smells, the fragrance of a roasting turkey.

I like the anticipation and excitement on the faces of the very young as they tell about the things they have requested from Santa. I like the knowing winks of the older children, letting you know that though they don't believe in Santa any more, they do not intend to spoil their little brother or sister's excitement.

I cherish the memory of the pot-holder, wooden stool and ceramic ashtray which at varying stages of my schooling, I made for my parents. I can still recall what appeared to be a sincere look of joy on their faces when they received these predictable presents.

I enjoy the letters and cards from people so far buried in the past that sometimes we have to probe the deep layers of memory to dredge up their faces. Not their present day faces – those we may never know – but their smiling unlined faces of years ago. It does one good to recall them and the happy times we once had together.

I enjoy the Christmas pantomimes, puddings and parties (at least some of them). I have little patience with those grimly spiritual people who react so violently against what the world has done to Christmas that they would simply have us all stand around and look pious. The God I believe in, is on the side of healthy fun and kindly laughter.

I enjoy the music of Christmas, carols sung out-of-doors on a frosty night, carols sung in a church or concert hall to the accompaniment of a mighty organ or orchestra. I remember once listening to a Salvation Army band in a crowded city street playing 'Hark the Herald Angels Sing' and 'O Come All Ye Faithful'. For a few moments I was lifted beyond my preoccupying business. I was Surprised by Joy. I could almost hear the angels sing.

I like the way that even hard cynical people can be caught off guard in a Christmas pageant and be melted by children singing 'Away in a Manger'.

I enjoy Christmas also because I value family gatherings. At a time when the family is under fierce attack, I am for anything that strengthens family ties. The health of any community or nation ultimately depends on the quality of its family life. What a joy it is at Christmas to see so many families reunited.

But there are deeper reasons why I value Christmas. At Christmas we celebrate a birth that changed the world. We celebrate a life that was lived, a life that transformed people's thinking about God, greatness, power and death, a life that deepened immeasurably the meaning of love, that gave qualities such as mercy, compassion, humility and forgiveness, a new place in the esteem of men and women. Many who encountered Jesus became better and kinder people. They in turn made the world a better and kinder place. Jesus has kindled more fires of affection, induced more liberality and compassion, and set in motion more poetry and song, and inspired more great art than any other person who ever lived. That first Christmas a new and powerful force for good entered the world. Jesus of Nazareth lit a great candle of hope in the midst of history.

I believe in Christmas because I don't want to forget, and I don't want others to forget the birth that changed the mental climate of the world. Tell me if you like, that Christmas is over commercialised – tell me that it goes back to the Saturnalia when the Roman child brought his teacher a present – tell me that it is closely linked to a nature festival commemorating the rebirth of longer days. I know all this, but I still want to retain Christmas. As well as commemorating the greatest single event in the history of the world, its message of peace on earth and goodwill towards all, is desperately needed by our embattled generation.

Nativity Plays

A 20th century innovation to the Christmas festivities, has been the reintroduction of the Nativity Play. Awestruck toddlers, dressed in brightly coloured dressing gowns or angel costumes, are herded down church aisles. From beside the Christmas tree in the chancel, they wave to their proud parents and grandparents packed into the church pews. Who does not feel a lump in the throat as they sing 'Away in a Manger' with beguiling innocence. To let a tear trickle down on such occasions is not sentimental. It is letting Christmas reach those parts of our emotions that other seasons of the year do not reach.

Unplanned and humorous things often happen in these nativity plays. For years thereafter, families will recall the night little Timmy screamed and ran to his parents, or how Tommy struck a shepherd on the head with the marble bag that represented the gold brought by one of the Wise men, or the time one of the angels fell off her pedestal, or how little Marie effectively eclipsed the rest of the choir as she belted out, 'Twinkle, twinkle, little star . . .'

During a nativity play in a Paisley school, a little girl with an attractive lisp narrated in her own words the old old story. 'Jesus was born in the middle of the night, and Mary woke up to see what was happening.' (I am sure Mary wished it had been as easy as that!) The second narrator then added, 'And that is why we sellotape Christmas.'

Nativity plays help swell congregations, but far more important they give children a feel for the Christmas story which they can never quite grasp in the classroom.

*   *   *

A teacher in London was called on to produce the school's nativity play. In spite of elaborate coaching and rehearsal, she felt fairly sure that the children would run dry on their lines sooner or later. This duly happened. Mary aged twelve and Joseph aged eleven, stood for some time in the centre of the stage in helpless silence, broken in the end by Mary stepping forward and thumping Joseph smartly in the ribs with the words, 'Wyke up Joe. I fink I'm goin' to 'ave a byeby.' Joseph's reaction to the news was less than enthusiastic: 'Cor, whatever next?'

Wallace Purling was nine years of age. Most people knew he was not very bright. He was big and clumsy, slow in movement and mind, but what a charming boy he was. Wally was liked by the other children, though the boys would sometimes get annoyed when Wally wanted to join in the ball games with them. Nobody wanted him in their team. Wally was a helpful boy, very willing and always smiling. He was the natural protector of the underdog. When the older boys used to chase the younger boys away, it was Wally who stuck up for them. 'Can't they stay? They're no bother.'

Christmas was approaching. Wally fancied being a shepherd with a flute in the nativity play, but the teacher gave him a more important role. She made him the inn-keeper. The inn-keeper did not have many lines to say and Wally's size would make his refusal of lodging to Joseph more forceful. On the night of the play, a large audience gathered. Wally stood in the wings watching all that was going on. Then Joseph appeared, slowly and tenderly guiding Mary. He knocked hard on the wooden door of the inn. Wally opened the door and said in a loud voice, 'What do you want?'

'We seek lodging,' said Joseph. 'Seek it elsewhere,' said Wally. 'The inn is full.' 'But sir, we have asked everywhere and we have travelled far and are weary.' 'There is no room in the inn for you,' said Wally looking very stern. 'But please good innkeeper, my wife is heavy with child. You must have some corner for her to rest.'

For the first time the innkeeper looked down at Mary. There then followed a very long pause. From the wings the audience could hear the teacher prompting, whispering, 'No, Begone.' Wally repeated the words, 'No, Begone.'

Joseph sadly placed his arm round Mary, and the two of them started to move away. Wally stood in the doorway watching. His mouth was open, his brow creased with concern. His eyes filled unmistakably with tears. Then suddenly this Christmas play became different from others. 'Don't go Joseph.' Wally called back. His face then broke into a smile. 'You can have my room.' Some of the boys and girls thought Wally had ruined the play. But many in the audience considered it the best Christmas play they had ever seen.

(Based on a story by Dina Donohue *Guideposts* Dec. 1966.)

Limping Angels

One more Christmas pageant! This must be number 101 for me. Sweet nativity plays, well produced ones, ridiculously awkward ones, and combinations of all of these, have been paraded before loving eyes of parents and grandparents at Christmas time. What is there new under the sun to be said by little children acting out the Christmas story? Shepherds in their brother's bathrobe and towel-turbans, wise men in gold-paper crowns carrying mother's jewellery, pixie angels in tinsel halos and foil wings, all kneeling before a box singing 'Silent Night' (slightly off-key).

From the start this pageant was different. I don't ever remember seeing shepherds roll up to a manger in wheelchairs or angels limp along to the heavenly chorus. This time the shepherds, angels and wise men were our cerebral palsied children. Did you ever try to dress in robe and halo a little one whose arms and legs jerked spastically in all directions? I was beginning to wonder if all this tremendous effort was going to be worth it. Three wise men in paper crowns, all arriving at the same time, came walking through parallel bars instead of riding on camels. Their gifts fairly leaped from spastic fingers to the baby's feet. Mary sat silently, arms folded across her blue robe, as with a faraway, wistful look in her eyes she hummed 'Away in a Manger'. She doesn't talk. The joy of one little shepherd was such that his arm flew awry and knocked his turban over one eye, but never has any shepherd been so glad to see the Babe in the manger. No smile has ever matched his in radiance as he tried to sing 'Away in a Manger'. Little angels with shining eyes under foil halos were singing, 'Joy to the world, the Lord has come!' – and somehow it seemed that they knew this joy and their Lord, this Baby Jesus.

Yes, I know it's the same old story, but this was not done in quite the same old way. If in all of this these little ones can know God's love and joy, why do I, so much older and wiser, doubt God's love and miss God's joy?

Yes, one more Christmas pageant. It was worth all the work involved, because, as one little shepherd sighed, 'It was a good Christmas story!'

Barbara Kirby.

*   *   *

The Alternative Pageant

Each year in film award ceremonies, the judges award Oscars for the best film, the best director, the best male or female performer. I am glad they also include an award for the best supporting character, for the success of any film depends not just on the few stars, but on the great cast of supporting characters. For the lead actor, applause, publicity and glory can be powerful motivating factors. It is much harder for those playing supporting roles to give of their best, for they are virtually ignored by the critics, and seldom applauded by the audience. The actor Charles Brookfield who was once erroneously reported dead, had the unusual experience of reading his own obituary. It said among other things, 'Never a great actor, he was invaluable in small parts.' I hope he took that as a tribute.

The traditional Christmas pageant about Mary, Joseph and the baby Jesus is staged each year in countless schools and churches. Less well known is the pageant of which Matthew speaks, the pageant of the many ordinary, little-known people, saints and sinners, who in the providence of God were ultimately responsible for the unique birth that took place in that Bethlehem manger – people like Uzziah, Jotham, Ahaz. It even includes some who did not belong to the chosen people – non Jews who were considered by many to be outcasts, like Ruth the Moabite. The genealogy also includes a few like Rahab whose names were seldom mentioned in respectable society. There may well have been skeletons rattling in the closets of some of the others as well.

One Christmas I was tempted to take as my sermon text the entire genealogy of Jesus as recorded in Matthew's Gospel. But I resisted, for it is so lengthy that I feared many might have gone to sleep before I got started on the actual sermon. Yet hidden away in that dull genealogy is one aspect of the good news of Christmas – how God can use one and two talented people like you and me, people even with tarnished lives, to bring something of his brightness to the world. In the sight of God ordinary people who play 'minor' roles well are tremendously important. Minor is our word, not God's. Just as in music there are no unimportant notes, so in God's sight there are no unimportant people.

* * *

People who depend on their family tree for status, should shake it first. Let us not forget that the one thing most family trees have in common are a few shady branches!

A young minister was called to a rural church. Being recently out of college with its heady theological discussions, he set up a series of lectures to deliver to his members on Thursday evenings. His first topic was, 'Immaculate Conception'. He gave what he imagined to be an inspired lecture on the subject. When he had finished he asked if there were questions, not really expecting any. A little old lady at the back raised her hand and inquired timidly, 'Uh, what are its advantages?'

Bethlehem Spectacular

In a Christmas meditation Richard E Wentz once depicted God announcing that the Time is come, that He would go even Now and be born in Bethlehem. Wentz then continues:

From countless depths there came reply,
'O Lord, how excellent! how fine!
That you should come to us.
Bethlehem shall give you proper claim.
The life of man shall greet you as befits your crown.
Abraham and Jacob's Department Store
Shall glisten and sparkle on Avenue Salem.
Their wares shall shout your Day
For weeks ahead.
Plastics, ribbons, lights, and blurbs,
Champagne, perfume, spice and herbs;
Music, gaiety, LP discs, and noise;
Ah, what magnificent, glorious build-up!
The streets we'll gild and trim and brighten
Especially where the sights are drab, the people shabby.
BORN! you say - a *real* birth?
That is full of human interest!
The magazines can carry 'shots' of the Expectant Mother
And perhaps add just a touch of glamour to the girl.
The father a carpenter? Well, we'll arrange a change!
A man of such import could be 'consultant'
To the architects' firm of Wright & Wright.
For weeks ahead we'll give direct TV report
To stir the public interest.

Follow eyewitnesses to the presidential suite
Of the Bethlehem Hilton
Where finest obstetricians and dutiful nurses
Will provide the most majestic care.
The office staffs of Trans Eastern Airlines,
Of Ishmael & Abimelech, of Nazareth Imports, Ltd.,
Will toast the day in festive mode.
Tickertape and limousine
Shall manifest the grandeur
And men shall give You thanks.
They shall honour You, worship You, O Lord!
The Bands will play, the people shout;
Climaxed-capped-and exalted
By a visit to the Grand Ballroom
Of the Bethlehem Hilton with dancing for all
And testimonies by mayors and chieftains,
Kings, presidents, governors
And all those things!
The Royal Couple – wined and dined,
Honoured and sped.
A Merry Christmas we'll call it! A Spectacle of Thanks!
A Spectacle for God! Spectacle in Bethlehem! Bethlehem Spectacular!'

THEN GOD SAID, 'Bethlehem! Bethlehem! How, oh, how long
Will you persist in justifying the power of power?
How long will you worship the big and the bright?
Why must you say, 'This is the way it should be'?
Your way is your sin – your spectacular *your* righteousness.
But I am gentle and lowly in heart.
I shall put down the mighty from their thrones
And exalt those of low degree.
A Saviour, the Lord your God.
Seek Him while He may be found.
Spread a simple table;
For He comes in bread and wine
And the cries of the despised and rejected.
No ballroom of honour and esteem;
Only the recovery room of an unnoticed stable.
SPECTACULAR, Yes! God's own Spectacle
In God's own time! In God's own design!
Bethlehem Spectacular!'

Family Parties

For me one of the great joys of a family Christmas is when we share an array of stories, particularly amusing stories of things that once happened to us. Some of the best fun times a family can have, occur when everybody sits round a table after a good meal and recalls old yarns and tales of bygone days. No other party is as good. Sometimes stories become embroidered, but it does not really matter for it is party time. Our family enjoys recalling how my wife once told an elderly teacher that the reason she had not been at the school dance was that she had been 'indecapitated'.

Also part of our family's shared narrative is the time when the family were at home from college for Christmas. There was a great deal of practical joking. My oldest son Neil was in the thick of it. Finally to get our own back, I switched off the hot water supply to the shower seconds after he had entered it. He emerged quicker than usual, but to the surprise of everyone said nothing. The following morning, however, just before I left for the B.B.C. studio in Inverness to play the role of Santa in a children's phone-in programme, he said, 'I think I will phone and see if Santa could give us a shower with hot-water.' The thought that he might just carry out his threat cast a shadow over the entire broadcast!

Recalling such incidents from the past makes for a greater sense of belonging, and creates a shared sense of history.

*　　*　　*

Home is the place where we are treated the best and grumble the most.

To a husband who was setting out to buy his wife's Christmas present, she said, 'Don't buy me anything practical. It's the impractical things I really need!'

Customer at Christmas to a television salesman: 'No, I don't need a remote control. With three teenagers my chances of controlling the set are already remote.'

Jane returned from the Christmas Sunday School party in the church which her parents had recently joined. She told her mother that the teacher had been asking about their family and whether she had any brothers and sisters. 'That was kind of her to take an interest in you,' said her mother. 'But it is strange,' said the girl, 'When I said I was an only child she said, 'Thank goodness'.'

There are some people who want to throw their arms around you simply because it's Christmas; there are other people who want to strangle you because it's Christmas.

Billy Graham described heaven as a family reunion that never ends. On hearing this, a T.V. comedian said he shuddered to think what hell must be like!

After a disastrous Christmas family get-together with both sets of in laws, a husband said to his wife, 'I will say one thing for your relatives. I much prefer your mother-in-law to mine.'

The problem with mixed marriages is not that he is Jewish and she is Gentile, or that he is British and she is Philippine. The problem is that he is a man and she is a woman.

It has been suggested that the reason God made man before woman is that God did not want any advice on how to make man.

The Christmas Dinner

Like the Roman festival of Saturnalia, Christmas in the Middle Ages was a time of great feasting. The reputed menu for King Arthur's Christmas dinner was 'venison, boars' heads, honey, mustard, mutton, beef, pork, herons, bitterns, peacocks, swans, bustards, teal, mallard, pigeons, widgeons, plum puddings, pancakes, apple pies and custard, not to mention wine, mead, ale and cider.' Quite a meal! Even if that were legend, later history does document a Christmas pie nine feet in circumference, weighing 168lbs. and containing twenty-nine game birds. The Christmas pies were so enormous that it became proverbial that 'the devil himself dare not appear in Cornwall during Christmas for fear of being baked in a pie.'

Ever since Dickens in his classic, *A Christmas Carol* made Scrooge mark his conversion by sending a turkey to the family of his poor clerk Bob Cratchit, turkey – like plum pudding, mince pies and Christmas cake – has become part of the traditional Christmas fare.

The turkey has had a bad press since it was domesticated. It quickly acquired the reputation of being a stupid creature. The phrase 'he is a real turkey' reinforces this dubious reputation. The early turkeys which were imported to Britain from Europe and America in the 16th century, were reared in Norfolk and Cambridgeshire. Before making the long journey to London, the turkey drovers would sometimes attach small leather boots to their feet to protect them on the journey. Others would tar the turkey's feet. Later the turkeys were slaughtered at the farm before being transported by stagecoach to London.

Today there are two problems commonly associated with the big Christmas turkey. Some home ovens are not big enough to cook them. And for days after Christmas, every culinary trick has to be used to dispose of the turkey left-overs – turkey patties, turkey rechauffé, turkey devilled, turkey fritters. Every time we open the refrigerator, turkey confronts us. Sometimes alongside it, is a half-eaten ham and portions of various cheeses.

A celebrated cook once listed ideas for the Christmas dinner left-overs – how to make a spicy turkey curry with red peppers and parsnips, how to transform the unused Stilton into a tasty nourishing soup, and how to purée the brussels sprouts. . . . Turkey with puréed brussels sprouts! The very thought would make me wish we had bought a smaller turkey and fewer brussels sprouts.

*   *   *

A teenage girl was overheard saying to her friend, 'My mother this Christmas put on weight because of shame – 'It's a shame to waste the rest of this. It's a shame to waste the rest of that.'

A young woman tells how her boyfriend invited her one Christmas to have a meal in the local three star hotel. As she scanned the menu, she noticed that most of the dishes that appealed to her were in the upper price range. With a glint in her eye she asked her boyfriend, 'How much do you love me?' After scanning the menu he replied, 'More than the turkey but not as much as the broiled lobster!'

At a popular American restaurant, renowned for its cuisine, two groups were enjoying a pre-Christmas lunch. One group consisted of local businessmen. For dessert they had requested watermelon soaked generously in brandy. The other group was a gathering of Presbyterian ministers. Their watermelon was to be without 'sauce'! But by mistake, the watermelon intended for the businessmen was served to the clergy. When the manager was informed of the mistake, he asked if the ministers had been upset? 'Well, put it this way,' said the waiter, 'They all saved the seeds and took them home for planting.'

A dieter is someone who wishes others would not laugh at his expanse.

A man who had read about an 'Eat all you want at Christmas' diet, later said to a friend. 'I knew there would be a catch in it. You have to jog seventeen miles a day.'

Can you remember when the Christmas Day meal was thought out carefully, not *thawed* out carefully.

Christmas desserts: 'A moment on your lips, a lifetime on your hips.'

At a Christmas party some years ago, a lady was suddenly aware of her husband advancing towards her accompanied by Lord Mountbatten. With unfortunate timing she had just put a hot vol-au-vent filled with lobster in a creamy sauce into her mouth. Summing up the situation, Lord Mountbatten smiled and said, 'I like a woman who is a good listener.'

Staggering into a bar, a drunk man shouted, 'Merry Christmas everyone!' The man closest to him said, 'You fool, it's the middle of February.' The bewildered drunk looked at him and cried, 'Oh my goodness. My wife is going to kill me. I've never been this late before.'

A lady explained that she knew she had had too much to drink when a 'little blurred tells me'.

When a society columnist asked a leading statesman how he arranged the seating for the notables who each year accepted invitations to his renowned Christmas lunch, he replied, 'I don't bother about who sits where. Those who matter don't mind, and those who mind don't matter.'

The Christmas cocktail party is a device for paying off obligations to people you don't want to invite to dinner!

Just prior to Christmas a minister answered his telephone to hear a lady's voice say, 'Could you send two cases of beer to my home?' The minister recognised the voice as being that of one of his members. He replied gently, 'It's your minister speaking.' Instead of the apology which he expected for dialling the wrong number, she retorted, 'What are you doing in the brewery?'

'One of the disadvantages of too much wine is that it makes a man mistake words for thoughts.'

It was not mere grumpiness which impelled Aldous Huxley to end his novel *The Genius and the Goddess* with one character saying to another, 'Drive carefully. . . . This is a Christian country and it is the Saviour's birthday. Practically everyone you see will be drunk.'

A man tells how after finishing an excellent meal at his favourite restaurant he decided to pay the bill with his credit card. While fumbling for his pen to sign the slip, the waiter pulled one out of his pocket. 'Here sir, use mine,' he said graciously, 'It has a bigger *tip*.'

The Christmas Rush

'The shepherds came with haste.' It has been suggested that they were the forerunners of the Christmas rush which unless carefully watched can make Christmas a nightmare. 'I wrap, send, clean, cook and worry that no one is left out,' said one woman. 'I worry about whether the money will spin out, whether the turkey will fit the oven, and how best to place the chairs round the festive table. I feel a tensioned goodwill to everyone.' Another flustered housewife complained of the 'clutter and confusion of Christmas'. Once the festive season is over, many find they are ninety days ahead with their calorie intake, and ninety days behind with their bills.

In the Gospel story about Martha and Mary who entertained Jesus at Bethany, Martha exhausted herself with much bustling and serving, while Mary sat at the feet of Jesus listening. Although Jesus said that of the two sisters, Mary had chosen the better part, the sympathy of the majority is with Martha. 'Lord,' she said, 'do you not care that my sister has left me to serve alone?' But Jesus answered, 'Martha, Martha, you are too anxious, too busy.'

Neither Martha nor Mary is perfect. We need the qualities of both. Christmas would lose much if we really managed to opt out of all the presents, entertaining and decorating. A hamburger on Christmas day without friends or relatives, would not be the same! But Christmas also loses much if like Martha we fail to make time to relax and worship, and ponder the deeper meaning of Christmas. Let us make sure all the rushing, cleaning, cooking and decorating does not destroy the peace, goodwill and joy which ought to characterise the festival of Christ's birth.

*   *   *

Nothing destroys the Christmas spirit more than looking for a place to park.

One thing about Christmas shopping is that it toughens you up for the Boxing Day sales!

A specialist in stress-related diseases points out the benefit of sometimes mentally blowing up a situation to the point of absurdity. If for example we are caught in a Christmas traffic jam, instead of fuming in silence, imagine the most awful scenario possible. 'These cars will never move. They will have to close the road and airlift us all out of here, one at a time. When they finally get to me, my children will have celebrated not only Christmas, but several other Christmases as well. They will have grown up motherless. They probably will not remember who I am.' By exaggerating the traffic jam situation to the point of ludicrousness we begin to laugh. Such a saving sense of humour can reduce blood pressure, heart rate and muscle tension.

What some adults want for Christmas is the day after.

A tongue in cheek article in the *Daily Mirror* once suggested '20 ways to stop going crackers' on Christmas Day. Directed at housewives on whom the burden of Christmas Day falls, it advocated among other things:

1. Resist the temptation to curse Christmas. Instead start cooking.

2. Say silently, 'This is the season of goodwill to all men, including his mother. . . .'

3. When the umpteenth member of the family has asked what is wrong with your face and why you're so miserable, pick up the telephone, ring British Airways and confirm a single booking on flight BA 257 from Heathrow to Barbados.

Christmas Cards

Up until the 1880s the sending of cards was confined mainly to the upper classes. Many of the designs on these early cards had little or no connection with the festive season. Pictures of naked nymphs and children were very popular. The development of cheaper methods of printing, and cheaper postage, finally made it possible for the majority to send cards. As the greeting card industry grew, the cards came to have a more Christmassy flavour.

At one time the Post office delivered mail on Christmas Day. In fact for some time it was customary for people to receive their cards on Christmas morning. But as the number of cards increased, this put an immense burden on the postal staff. By the end of the 19th century people were being urged to post their cards in advance. These cards were then sorted, but held for delivery on Christmas morning. This scheme lasted for about six years in some towns, but with the volume of cards ever increasing it finally had to be stopped. Millions of Christmas cards are now sent every year.

A Christmas card from a distant friend of long standing, or a card with a newsy letter included, can often be like a little bit of paradise coming through the mail. On the other hand there can be few things more depressing than an empty letter box at Christmas.

*   *   *

As a friendly postman delivered the Christmas mail he paused to chat with a four-year-old about his baby sister. 'Can she talk?', the postman asked. 'No,' said the little fellow, 'she has a few teeth but her words have not come in yet.'

In October we are told 'Post Early for Christmas'. But as Robert Morley pointed out, if everybody did this, in the days just before Christmas, the Post Office would have hundreds of postmen and women sitting round thinking the sorting machines had broken down.

In a rush of last minute Christmas shopping, a woman bought a box of fifty identical greeting cards. Without bothering to read the verse she hastily signed and addressed all but one of them. Several days after they had been posted, she came across the one card left. Looking at the message she was horrified to read, 'This card is just to say, A little gift is on the way.'

An early Christmas card,

A Glasgow youngster at the Christmas card counter was overheard to say to a friend, 'They're no Christmas cairds, they're holy yins.'

The world's biggest Christmas card was painted by Qantas Airlines on the side of one of their Boeing 707s. 'HAVE A QANTASTIC CHRISTMAS.'

Christmas Cards

There is a list of folks I know
All written in a book,
And every year at Christmas time
I go and take a look.
And that is when I realize that
These names are a part,
Not of the book they're written in
But of my very heart.

For each name stands for someone
Who has touched my life sometime,
And in that meeting they've become
The 'Rhythm of the Rhyme'.
I really feel I am composed
Of each remembered name,
My life is so much better
Than it was before you came.

So never think my Christmas cards
Are just a mere routine
Of names upon a list,
Forgotten in between.
For when I send a Christmas Card
That is addressed to you
It is because you're on that list
Of folks I'm indebted to.

And whether I've known you
For many years or few,
In some way you had a part
In shaping things I do.
So every year when Christmas comes
I just realise anew
The biggest gift that God can give
Is knowing folks like you!

Anon.

A Letter to Santa

Shortly after the Second World War, there was a man who worked in the post office. He was known as 'the dead letter man' because he handled letters with vague or faulty addresses. He had a lovely wife, a daughter Marion and a tiny son. He was a happy person. Often after supper he would light his pipe and tell them about his exploits in delivering lost letters. Then suddenly one May his little boy died. His wife and daughter struggled to control their grief. Not so the father. He withdrew into himself. He never laughed.

As Christmas approached his depression intensified. His wife told him that such despair was unfair to their lost son and to Marion. But it made no difference. Then one day he saw on top of the 'difficult to deliver' pile of letters a P.C. addressed to Santa Claus, North Pole. He paused to read it.

'We are very sad at our house this year. My brother died and my Daddy is terribly upset. I wonder if you could give Daddy something that would make him like he used to be; make him smoke his pipe again and tell me stories. I heard Mummy say that only Eternity could cure him. If you could bring him some of that, I will promise to be a good girl.

Marion.

That night he walked home faster. Outside the back door he lit his pipe. Then he walked in and blew a great puff of smoke. When his wife and Marion looked up, he smiled warmly as he used to do.

No Place Like Home

I am glad there are still many homes where in the climate of confidence little girls blossom out from shy wall-flowers, where parents give extra care to the child that is not so good looking or talented, and are prepared to make sacrifices for a crippled son who will never be able to pay them back. I am glad there are family circles where we can escape from the cutting edge of competition and enjoy the grace of cooperation.

During General Allenby's campaign against the Turks, a unit of Scottish troops was on patrol in the desert. Suddenly they dived for cover. Up ahead they saw something white fluttering among the scrub. They immediately imagined an ambush. But when two of their unit wormed their way forward to investigate they found nothing more sinister than a wind-blown page from the *Hamilton Advertiser*. Nobody knows how it reached that desolate spot, but to the Lanarkshire lad who found it, that dog-eared page of newsprint was a welcome reminder of his family in Hamilton who seemed so far away. It was symbolic of those precious things for which home and family stood. For many years it hung in a glass frame in the *Hamilton Advertiser* office.

A friend of John Buchan was out visiting the wounded in Mesopotamia during the First World War. Passing from one bed to another, he came upon a Scots lad whose boyhood had been spent in Rothiemurchus, a small village nestling at the foot of the glorious Cairngorms. When Buchan's friend asked the lad where in the battlefield he had received his wounds, he replied, 'It was twa miles on the Rothiemurchus side o' Baghdad.' Far from his native-land, his boyhood home was never far from his thoughts.

Angels

There is a popular song in which someone is said to talk like an angel. Many of us have known such people. 'Come away in. Sit down while I make a cup of tea, and then tell me all about it.' 'Oh you are an angel,' we say.

Many times people have done for me the kinds of things that angels are said to do. They have encouraged me. They have offered me wise counsel. They have generously shared with me the material things of life. I never thought they were angels. They certainly did not look like the angels portrayed in stained glass with soft flowing garments and two large feathered wings. In fact they often did not even look angelic.

On Christmas Eve a father took his little girl to hospital to visit her mother. Now in the hospital it was the custom for the nurses to make their way round the wards with candles singing Christmas carols. The little girl seeing the nurses in their white uniforms asked if they were angels. In a very real sense they were, responding as they did with their hearts and hands, to the needs of patients.

*   *   *

The expression 'the voice of an angel' started me wondering what an angel sounds like. So I did some research, and discovered that an angel's voice is remarkably like a person saying 'Hurry Up'. Until the time I undertook the research I had thought the voice of an angel would always be beautiful. The words 'Get up' are rarely beautiful, never less so than at seven o'clock in the morning. Yet that is what angels say when they talk to people, as reported in the Bible. An angel comes to Peter in jail and says, 'Rise quickly.' An angel appears to Joseph in a dream when Herod is slaughtering the infants and says, 'Go quickly.' An angel appears to Philip and says 'Arise and go.' Listen carefully and you can hear the voice of angels above the contemporary din of the world, a voice that ought to get us out of easy chairs and comfortable beds. 'Arise, go quickly. There is much to be done.'

(Halford Luccock in the *Christian Century*.)

Wouldn't it be grand to be an angel
and have as your address:
'The Realms of the Glory of God.'
And swing on rainbows and
gather stars in your pockets,
winging in and out of the earth
in a flurry of moondust
with the messages of God?
Comforting the distressed,
encouraging the righteous,
delivering the just, guarding
little children. . . .
But all of us could do that.
We could comfort and encourage
and deliver and guard. . . .
Maybe if we can get that right,
we can swing on rainbows later. . . .
                                        Anon.

BLACK ANGELS

Last Christmas (1993) a newspaper headline read: 'Blacks in South Africa dream of last white Christmas.' That headline reminded me of a delightful African story told by General Eva Burrows, a former leader of the Salvation Army. Early on in her life she had been a teacher in a small mission station. As Christmas approached they started rehearsing for a Nativity play. The main characters had been chosen – Mary, Joseph and the Wise Men. There were to be eight angels. Six were black, but two were blonde, the daughters of a Norwegian couple who worked at the mission station. During the dress rehearsal Eva Burrows was back-stage with the angels. They all looked 'angelic' in their tinselled haloes, white robes and wings. Their shining countenances told her they were all thoroughly enjoying being dressed up in this way.

During a pause in the rehearsal, Eva Burrows heard one of the little Norwegian girls saying to her sister, 'Do you think there will be black angels in heaven?' 'Of course there will,' replied her older sister. 'Anyhow, Jesus would not know the difference.'

Would that we were all colour-blind in this respect.

ENTERTAINING ANGELS

The Bible not only encourages us to love one another, but also to welcome strangers. The writer of the letter to the Hebrews points out that some who have done this, have entertained angels unawares.

Most of the angels I have met, I have encountered first as strangers. Only later did I discover they possessed those characteristics that convinced me they had been sent by God. I recognised them as the kind of friends I would never want to be without. For Paul, Titus was such an angel. The apostle later wrote of him: 'God comforted me by the coming of Titus.' Most of us could think of someone of whom we could say much the same. 'God comforted me by the coming of . . . '.

There are many angels who initially look more like strangers than one might think. So the next time you meet a stranger extend a warm greeting. Who knows if an angel might be about?

And there were in the same country shepherds abiding in the fields, keeping watch over their flock by night. And the angel of the Lord shone round about them; and they were sore afraid. And the angel said unto them, 'Fear not, for behold I bring you good tidings of great joy, which shall be to all people. For unto you is born this day in the city of David a Saviour which is Christ the Lord. And this shall be a sign unto you, you shall find the babe wrapped in swaddling clothes, lying in a manger. And suddenly there was with the angel a multitude of the heavenly host praising God and saying, 'Glory to God in the highest, and on earth peace, goodwill toward men.'

In Luke's account of *the* event in history, the coming into the world of One who split history into before and after, fact and interpretation of fact, history and theology are inextricably interwoven. This is not surprising for facts that shed no light on the real meaning of the fact are always less than facts. Orientals were fortunately not cursed with our literal minds. They were artists with words. They knew that life's deepest experiences are often best expressed in word pictures. For Jews the all-important question about any story was 'what does this story teach?' They knew that word pictures and poetry often take us nearer to life's greatest truths than hard logical prose. Symbolism being the gateway to the human imagination, Luke clothed his description of the birth of Jesus in the language, metaphors and images of his day. Whereas for example we might speak of precious 'God-moments', or of a divine whisper in Mary's heart that 'her baby was very special', the Biblical writers depict angels speaking to Mary. In many other Biblical stories angels are depicted as being present where God was thought to be especially present.

I am certain the birth stories in Matthew and Luke describe the reality of God's entrance into human history more powerfully than any purely factual historian could have done. These stories which were written many years after that momentous birth in Bethlehem, remind us how both wise and simple, the shepherds and the wise men, found in Jesus of Nazareth the answer to many of their deepest longings and questions. The angelic chorus, 'Peace on earth, goodwill to men' highlights two of the major themes of Jesus' ministry. What a magnificent commentary these Christmas stories are on the faith of Matthew and Luke that in the life of Jesus the mind and heart of God had been revealed more clearly than anywhere else.

*   *   *

One Christmas Eve, when still extremely young and with a mind full of Christmas carols and quiring angels, I slipped into the garden under the leafless apple tree boughs, across the grass to my favourite haunt under the

53

big cherry tree. The windows of the distant houses beyond the fields were dimly lit, but in the sky above me were myriads of stars, beautiful beyond words, glorious. Everything was very still as if the earth waited. 'Please God, hurry up and make the angels sing,' I said. But the heavens were mute. The stars possibly hymned in their lonely star paths, but neither they nor the angels filled the heavens with praise. 'I think you might make the angels sing NOW', I said to God to whom I chatted often, especially when I wanted something very much. 'You know I shouldn't be out and I haven't my coat on. You know how they will go on if they find me here.' 'They' were my parents, not the angels. But not a treble note came from any angel. God was apparently on my parents' side as usual. I decided that out of sheer cussedness these temperamental angels would probably sing when I was asleep.

Meta Wright.

In church nativity plays, the little angels in their home-made white costumes, often look as if butter would not melt in their mouths. Yet I have also known teachers, prior to the start of the play having to referee fights between angels.

A friend's earliest memory was of her mother lifting her up to put the angel at the top of the Christmas tree. How much more attractive the angel looks when the lights are switched on.

The reason angels can fly is that they take themselves so lightly.

A teacher smiled when she read in a child's version of the Christmas story: 'The first angel appeared to tell Mary she was pregurunt, but Mary had already noticed.'

A saintly woman once asked her minister to explain the difference between those angelic creatures that the church calls cherubim and those that are called seraphim. Quick wittedly the pastor replied, 'Well ma'am, they did have a difference once, but they made it up.'

Heaven decided to send an angel to two Irishmen Murphy and Kelly who were bitter rivals. An angel was sent to pacify Murphy. 'Listen Murphy, you are very bitter and cold and cruel towards Kelly; to cure you the good Lord has promised to give you one of anything in the world that you want if only you will let Kelly have two of them.' Murphy thought for a moment than said, 'If I was to choose to be the head of one labour union would that mean that Kelly would be the head of two labour unions?'
'Yes' said the angel.
'And if I win the Irish sweepstake once, Kelly will win it twice?'

The angel said, 'That's right.'
'And I suppose it means that if I have a brass band following me, that Kelly will have one following him and one playing before him?'
'Yes.'
Murphy thought about it and said, 'Angel, I will choose a glass eye.'

Wife to minister who was eyeing the waiter in a restaurant. 'Let him snigger. If you want angel cake, you have it.'

I don't know the origin of the expression 'holy terror' but it is one my mother often used. I reserve it for those children who drive you up the wall and then fetch you down with an angelic smile.

A baby is an angel whose wings decrease as his legs increase.

Xmas

Xmas is a form of Christmas often frowned on as being slang and disrespectful. Many who think thus do not realise that X was the ancient sign of Jesus. The early Christians, who were often persecuted for their faith, were fond of such rubrics as X, IHS (a Latin misrendering of the first three letters of the Greek word for Jesus IESOUS), and ICHTHUS the Greek word for fish, another early symbol for Christ. So to write Xmas is not being disrespectful to him whose birth we celebrate. It puts one rather in the company of the early martyrs.

Messiah

For many people the word Messiah is more often associated with Handel's majestic oratoric than with the title for Jesus meaning 'Anointed', 'Deliverer', 'Saviour'. Likewise the word Benedictine is now more closely associated with the trade mark of a liqueur than an order of monks within the Roman church. Luke Eberle of the Order of St Benedict tells how when he and a Father Hubert returned to the United States from Europe, the customs officer pointed to a small bag which father Hubert was carrying. 'What have you in there, Father?' he asked courteously. 'Only an old Benedictine habit,' replied the soft spoken Father. Understandably the customs officer enquired, 'How many bottles?'

Advent

Advent is the name given to the four-week period leading up to Christmas. The word comes from the Latin meaning 'coming' or 'arrival'. Advent is the time when the church and individuals prepare for the festival of the Nativity. It is a time for reflection. A time for anticipation. A time for worship. It is a time for reading again the familiar words and hearing again the familiar stories.

The traditional Advent wreath is made of evergreen foliage – a reminder that in the darkness of winter there is still the promise of life. The wreath has four candles placed round a circular arrangement of evergreens or holly. On each of the four Sundays of Advent one of the candles is lit. The fifth and larger candle (usually white) is lit on Christmas Eve, to signify the birth of Christ, the 'Light of the world'. It also serves as a reminder that 'it is better to light a candle than curse the darkness.'

Purple and red are the most common colours for the four candles, purple symbolising royalty, humility and penitence, red symbolising the blood of Christ shed on the cross. The circular wreath represents the never-ending divine love, and the infinity of God's creation which God so loves. In some homes when the advent candle is lit before dinner, a carol is sung for grace.

The Chinese invented and used candles in their lanterns 5000 years ago. Since then candles have been used not only to provide light, but for decoration during special religious festivals. When Solomon built his temple he placed in it several golden candlesticks. Today in many continents, Christmas services are held in the glow of candlelight. The soft soothing light of candles fits in well with the mystic appeal of Advent and Christmas.

Many candles can be lit from one candle without diminishing it.

Waxing Lyrical

Emerging from a tentative foray into the Christmas shopping skirmish, I found myself pondering one of life's imponderable mysteries; what happens to all the fancy candles you see in fancy candle shops?

It cannot have escaped your notice that there are more fancy candles on the face of the earth than there are grains of sand, and that they are proliferating like tallow maggots. Wherever a new row of shops is opened, one of them will be a fancy candle shop. Show me a disused flower market or engine shed that is being converted into a brick-paved arcade and I will show you what that arcade is going to consist of: fancy candle shops.

These fancy candles come in the form of golf-balls, Christmas puddings, dogs, cats and other animals, telephone boxes, ice-cream cones, cartoon characters, dominoes and every type of fruit except strained prunes. Some of them even come in the form of candles. They are bought by the billion. Yet where do they all go? No one ever lights them. They are never placed in cottage windows to guide home wandering sailors. They are not used as wax ornaments or paperweights. They do not get eaten by Eskimos. Where are they? My belief is that one of these Christmases there will be a sudden and sickening sound of splintering wood throughout the land as the floorboards of millions of attics give way and millions of cupboard doors are forced off their hinges and a great tidal wave of fancy candles will roar down staircases and across living room carpets until every last jack of us has been buried by the blessed things.

This year I am giving everybody matches.

Keith Waterhouse, Daily Mirror.

Hello, little one.

Holly and Mistletoe

For centuries evergreens, those plants which do not lose their foliage in the winter, were regarded by pagan faiths as symbols of life. Holly, bearing as it does red berries even in the dead of winter, became a popular decorative shrub. Holly was hung in houses to bring occupants good luck and lasting life. Not surprisingly the church purloined holly as a powerful Christian symbol. The sharp pointed leaves symbolised the crown of thorns. The red berries represented the drops of blood where the crown of thorns pierced. In Denmark holly is known as 'Christ-thorn'.

Mistletoe was regarded by the Druids as a sacred healing plant. Perhaps because of its pagan associations, it was from earliest times banned from churches. A Breton legend tells how mistletoe was originally a tree, the timber of which was used for the cross. Thereafter out of shame it shrunk to a feeble parasitic shrub. The pagan rite of kissing under the mistletoe is very ancient. Dickens in his book *Sketches by Boz*, describes a family Christmas where the grandfather produces a small sprig of mistletoe from his pocket and tempts the young cousins to kiss under it. The mistletoe was often hung inside the door of the house. Every time a visitor to the house was kissed, one of the berries was removed from the sprig. When all the berries had gone the kissing had to stop.

Crackers and Mince Pies

Crackers were a variation of the ancient fire festivals. The story goes that a London sweet manufacturer Tom Smith was inspired one Christmas day to invent the cracker as he sat by a log fire which happened to be sparking. He had previously increased his sale of sweets by putting love-notes in with them. It occurred to him that day that perhaps he could also increase sales of his sweets at Christmas if he could somehow make them go bang. He experimented and finally succeeded in making a controlled explosion. His 'fire-cracker sweets' were a great success. Sales further increased when he added paper hats and trinkets, and 'punny' jokes.

The Christmas pie was originally oblong in shape, symbolising a crib. A small pastry baby representing Jesus was placed on the pie. Because this delicacy outraged the Puritans, the shape and name of the pie was changed. It became round instead of crib-shaped, and was referred to as a 'Minc'd Pie'. In Tudor times there was a saying, 'Eat one mince pie every day from Christmas to Twelfth Night and you will be happy for the rest of the year.'

Christmas Toys

In toy shops at Christmas the temptation is strong to buy on impulse. Asking the following questions before actually making a purchase could result in wiser choices.

1. Can I afford this toy? If you can't, but buy it anyway, you will probably not only feel guilty later, but may well communicate to your child something of your inner tension. 'Behave yourself. Think of the sacrifice I made to buy you that.'

2. Does this toy enable you to be part of the gift? A game which a young child can play with his parents can strengthen the bonds between them. 'Building toys' like Lego are better with an adult to start things off. And puppets need an audience!'

3. Does this toy allow the child to be in control? A car that runs only under child power, and costs a fraction of the price of a complex battery operated one, can sometimes offer more opportunity for imagination. It goes up the arm of the chair, turns into a rocket ship and flies to the moon. One educationalist puts it thus: 'Though batteries can add something to a car, they can also take away something from a young child.'

4. Will this toy encourage or discourage the child's social development? Social play being important for a child's development, at least some of the child's toys should be the kind that they can share with other youngsters.

5. Is this toy dangerous? As doting relatives we are accustomed to checking toys for sharp edges and little pieces which a child might swallow. But what of the psychological damage to a child? If we always buy the most expensive train set, or skis, or bicycle, are we unwittingly communicating the idea that happiness depends on getting the most expensive toys? That idea is quite false. One man tells how as a boy, he and a friend got tremendous enjoyment out of trying to mend some of the broken toys thrown out from wealthy homes. Looking back on these happy times, he wondered if the 'privileged' children who were overwhelmed with new expensive toys at Christmas, got as much fun from actually playing with them.

*   *   *

A three-year-old child gets almost as much fun out of a £50 toy as he does out of finding a caterpillar.

Christmas is when we celebrate the birth of the Prince of Peace by giving our kids machine guns and tanks.

An unbreakable Christmas toy is one that is guaranteed to last until the New Year.

Notice in toy shop window after Christmas: 'Sale! Inflatable toys – *slashed beyond belief.*'

The Toy's Tale

Margery Williams in her delightful book, *The Velveteen Rabbit*, tells of a Christmas toy rabbit who learns from an old rocking horse the secret of life. 'What is *Real*?', asked the rabbit one day, when they were side by side near the nursery fender. 'Does it mean having things that buzz inside you and a stick-out handle?'
'*Real* isn't how you are made,' said the rocking horse. 'It is a thing that happens to you. When a child loves you for a long, long time, not just to play with, but really loves you, then you become real.'
'Does it hurt?' asked the rabbit.
'Sometimes,' said the rocking horse, for he was always truthful. 'When you are real you don't mind being hurt.'
'Does it happen all at once, like being wound up,' he asked, 'Or bit by bit?'
'It does not happen all at once,' said the rocking horse. 'It takes a long time. That's why it doesn't often happen to people who break easily, or have sharp edges, or who have to be carefully kept. Generally, by the time you are *Real*, most of your hair has been loved off and you get loose in the joints and very shabby. But these things don't matter at all, because once you are *Real*, you can't be ugly, except to people who don't understand.'

Christmas Past

It was in the dead of night that the shimmering, child-like ghost of Christmas Past appeared out of the darkness by Scrooge's bedside to lead him on a mysterious journey. And yet, in a strange way, it was all so familiar.
'He was conscious of a thousand odours floating in the air, each one connected with a thousand thoughts, and hopes, and joys, and cares, long forgotten. . . .
'You recollect the way?' inquired the Spirit. 'Remember it!' cried Scrooge with fervour, 'I could walk it blind fold.'
And so, I suppose, could most of us, as we look backward into the past. There

is something special about this season of the year.

My impression is that whereas other days and other recollections seem to telescope and merge and fade, bygone Christmases remain clear milestones in my memory.

The breathless childhood excitement of discovering parcels at the foot of the bed in the early morning dark; Christmas Eve at sea in the crowded fo'c'sles of naval patrol boats; trying to find some festive cheer in blitzed and blacked-out London; singing carols in the steaming heat of Florida swamps; standing beside the coffin of my father as the church bells pealed out their message of goodwill, and every house seemed full of joy save ours; sharing at midnight in these strange and wonderful services when out of the dark streets the people come in their thousands, pouring into the churches to keep their annual truce in the House of God and bring their homage to the Christ-child.

Nelson Gray.

Christmas in the Trenches

In 1914 a moving incident took place on the Western Front. Although the British officers had made no arrangements for the British soldiers to celebrate Christmas in the trenches, the soldiers themselves had gathered bits of holly to decorate their dug-outs. The German soldiers on the other hand were provided with small Christmas trees as well as food parcels. On Christmas Eve – the high point of Christmas for Germans – the British soldiers were confronted with an extraordinary sight. Graham Williams describes what happened during his period on sentry duty.

'I was standing gazing out, and I thought what a different Christmas this was going to be from any I'd ever had before. I thought that my family back home would be putting up their decorations as they always did after supper on Christmas Eve, and my father would be thinking about making his rum punch. At exactly midnight German time, I suddenly saw lights appear in front of me all along the German trenches. I was wondering what was happening, and they started singing *Stille Nacht*, Silent Night. I'd not heard it before, and I thought what a beautiful tune it was.'

That was the start of an unofficial truce on the Western Front, during which British and German soldiers exchanged cigarettes and food, and even buttons from their uniforms as souvenirs. They showed each other pictures of their families, and posed for photographs standing in No-Man's land with arms embraced. Later that day a football match was suggested. One of the Germans had received a football as a Christmas present.

Carol singing in the German trenches.

The unofficial armistice did not however meet with official approval. Opposing soldiers who had embraced each other were moved back so that battle could recommence. A Bruce Bairnsfather who was present, describes the ending of the truce. 'I was suddenly sent for by the captain of my company. I arrived at his dug-out and heard that there was displeasure in the mind of the colonel at the proceedings. The news had reached the general and sharp orders had arrived to terminate any fraternisation immediately. What else can a General do? Chatting with the enemy has no place in his profession. So the officers began herding the soldiers back. Rifles soon spat forth death across the shell scarred turnip fields, banishing the spirit of Christmas that had flirted in a strange way across No Man's Land, and for a few hours had triumphed.'

* * *

During the war two striking drawings depicting a communal air-raid shelter, appeared in a newspaper. The first was of a well-to-do gentleman chatting with a poor lady during an air-raid. The second picture showed him speaking sternly to her. 'How dare you speak to me. Don't you know the air-raid is over?'

Partridge in a Pear Tree

For almost three hundred years after the Reformation, Roman Catholics in Britain were forbidden by law to practise their faith openly. The only way they could pass on their religion to their young people without arousing the fury or even the suspicions of their Protestant neighbours, was to put their teachings into a sort of code which would sound harmless to those who chanced to overhear it. 'Green grow the rushes o' was one of their 'catechism' songs. But the best example is a song which is a great favourite at most carol concerts at Christmas – 'The Twelve Days of Christmas'. 'On the first day of Christmas my true love sent to me, a partridge in a pear tree. . . .'

The 'twelve days' extend from 25 Dec. to 6 Jan., the date the church chose to mark the visit of the Wise Men to Bethlehem. The speaker is an ordinary Christian. God is the 'true love' who keeps sending gifts.

The first gift is a **Partridge in a pear tree**. To artists of the Middle Ages, a mother partridge symbolised Christ, the greatest of all God's gifts.

The **Two turtle doves** remind us of the sacrifice made by Mary and Joseph when Jesus was born. Not being able to afford a lamb, they were obliged to sacrifice two doves.

Three French hens. Because they were highly valued for their beauty. French hens were very costly. For some the three French hens symbolised the three costly gifts of the Wise Men, for others the three priceless virtues, faith, hope and love.

The **Four calling birds** suggest the Four Gospels.

Five gold rings. These are the only symbols in the song which lack life and movement. They are thought to have represented either the first five books of the Old Testament which contained the Sacred Law, or the five obligatory sacraments of the Roman Church.

Six geese a-laying. These ungainly but very productive creatures, suggest the six days of Creation.

Seven swans a swimming. These elegant birds represented the seven works of mercy.

Eight maids a-milking. These maids, providing vital nourishment for everyday life, suggest the eight Beatitudes – Blessed are the merciful, Blessed are the Peace-makers. . . . Christ's prescription for a fulfilled life.

Nine ladies dancing. These graceful dancers suggest the nine graceful fruits of the spirit as listed by St Paul – love, joy, peace, patience, kindness, goodness, fidelity, gentleness and self-control.

Ten lords a-leaping match up with the Ten Commandments.

Eleven pipers piping suggest the eleven disciples left to announce to the world the good news of the Resurrection, Judas having hung himself.

Twelve drummers drumming. Some believe they stand for the twelve Minor Prophets, but others maintain they referred to the twelve points of belief in the Apostles Creed.

Thus Roman Catholics in the 17th and 18th centuries passed on to their young people some of the basic components of their faith. The interesting 'accumulative pattern' to the song, each verse adding some new gift and then working its way back through those gifts already mentioned, serves as a reminder of the way in which God, not only bestows fresh gifts on us, but keeps renewing gifts previously given.

(Based on an article by Hugh Mckellar in the *Observer*, the official magazine of the United Church of Canada. Dec. 1978)

I Want Some More

While the television crew were setting up their lights and cameras for an interview to be included in an Advent 'Highway' programme, Sir Harry Secombe and I had the opportunity to chat and share anecdotes. When I commented on the personal motto on his signet ring 'Go on', he laughed and said, 'You can read it as "Goon" if you like!' When Sir Harry laughs, it is as though his whole body is having a massage.

That day in Skibo Castle, Sir Harry shared with me a delightful story about the making of the musical *Oliver*, a film which has become very much part of Christmas television viewing. In the musical Sir Harry plays Mr Bumble, the superintendent of the orphanage.

The signal had been given for Oliver to rise from the orphanage dining table, and go to where Mr Bumble was standing. As Sir Harry looked into little Oliver's angelic face, and heard him say in a pleading tone, 'Please sir, I want some more?', his heart melted, and his irrepressible sense of fun took over. He tapped Oliver on the head and said, 'Sure', and put another dollop of porridge into his plate. Had Sir Harry not been a close friend of the producer, he might have got the sack there and then. The scene had to be done all over again.

The following morning they filmed Mr Bumble dragging Oliver by the ear out of the workhouse and into the street. Though Sir Harry felt the first 'take' had gone well, the producer informed him they would have to do it again, for not sufficient pain had been registering on Oliver's face. 'You will have to pull Oliver's ear until it really hurts,' said the producer. Though reluctant to inflict such pain, he felt that, having messed up the previous day's filming, he had better do what he was told. So at the appropriate moment he grabbed Oliver by the ear and really tugged. His heart missed a beat when the ear suddenly came away in his hand. Unknown to him, the producer, determined to get his own back on Harry, had instructed the make-up team to fit a false ear!

*   *   *

Another stage production which has become an integral part of the Christmas festivities is James Barrie's *Peter Pan*. When asked at a dinner party how he managed to write so many successful plays, Barrie replied, 'My plays are not all successes. Some Peter out and some Pan out.'

A television engineer Hugh Cochrane tells how he was called out one Christmas to the home of the local doctor. He found the doctor's ten-year-old television set to be in very poor condition. He had just finished checking its many faults when the doctor said in his professional manner. 'After your diagnosis what do you prescribe?' Hugh looked at him thoughtfully for a few moments before saying, 'A post-mortem'.

In the Bleak Mid-Winter

In the bleak mid-winter
Frosty winds made moan
Earth stood hard as iron
Water like a stone.

It had been like that for days. The local forecast, which was usually reasonably accurate, had predicted a further heavy snow-fall. The result was that the local supermarket was even more crowded than usual, customers braving sub-zero temperatures to stock up with supplies for the festive season. Tempers were becoming frayed. The shopping trolleys were all in use. The check out queues were exceptionally long.
One elderly man, who seemed to be unaware that there was a separate check-out for those purchasing less than six items, waited without complaint in one of the long queues to pay for two items. His turn finally came. As the girl rang up his two purchases, those nearby suddenly fell silent, for the old man had braved the crowds, the icy roads, the traffic chaos and the freezing temperatures to buy a large bag of bird seed and a large packet of nuts, both for his feathered friends. The horizon of his concern extended beyond food for himself.

*   *   *

Fiona Dalton tells how she sent a Christmas pudding to some French friends. She placed the traditional sprig of holly on top before wrapping up the parcel. A few weeks later she received a doleful letter. 'Thank you so much for the plant. We watered it every day, but unfortunately it died.'

A Sigh of Belief

Sometimes by taking a familiar phrase and changing a single letter, one can make it even more memorable.

Nothing is so humiliating as tripping over your own feat.

Sixty is when actions begin to creak louder than words.

Beauty involves making the best of one's good paints.

My own favourite concerns Christmas.

At Christmas the world breathes a great sigh of belief.

I wish that were true more often. Unfortunately many of us get so engrossed in the other aspects of Christmas – the writing, wrapping, mailing, meals – that the all important *belief* side is forgotten.

The longer I am in the ministry the more convinced I become of the importance of what people believe. I am not thinking of what they profess to believe in church, or what they would like to believe, but of what they really do believe in their heart of hearts about God and goodness, giving and getting, life and death. These beliefs make us the people we are.

Our Christmas celebrations and our lives could be enriched if, as well as enjoying the Christmas dinner, the family parties and the pantomime, more people would breathe a great 'sigh of belief':

— the belief that the maker of heaven and earth once walked this earth as the poor person's friend.
— the belief that Jesus is the starting point for learning what life is all about.
— the belief that we are here, not to fight for our own advantage, but to do something beautiful for God.
— the belief that caring love is the best way of all.
— the belief that our one or two talents do matter in the cosmic scheme of things.
— the belief that there is nothing in life or death that can ever separate us, or our loved ones from the love of God.

No Room at the Inn

Many of us were brought up to think of the Bethlehem inn-keeper as a heartless, mean soul who deliberately decided to relegate a poor couple to what the carols call 'a stable bare'. Without any real evidence we have been fiercely critical of the inn-keeper.

The little town of Bethlehem, being one of the designated 'taxing centres', would be bursting at the seams that momentous night. The inn-keeper, who is not mentioned in the Gospel narratives, would almost certainly have no spare accommodation. He could have left it there. Yet apparently such was his concern, or his wife's concern, for Mary and Joseph, that they improvised a bed in the manger. The manger was not as many think, a barn or stable. It was the lower section of the house where the family's few animals were kept at night, and where the family often lived. It is worth noting that Matthew tells us that when the Wise Men arrive, 'they went into the house', not some out-house.

Accustomed as many of us are in the West to spotlessly clean labour suites, and centrally heated accommodation, the birth of a baby with cattle looking on naturally startles us. But let us not forget that situated as the manger was just off the main living room, it would be the warmest place in the house. It can also be very comfortable to nestle down in fresh hay.

We shall never know the whole truth about the inn-keeper. Just because an inn-keeper lives by charging for hospitality, he is often unfairly denied the reputation he deserves. The inn-keeper may well not have charged Mary and Joseph. Hotel keepers do on occasions give free hospitality to deserving cases. But even then they don't always get the credit they deserve. Some are sure to point out that they charge it up to advertising. In Chaucer's *Canterbury Tales*, when the host of the Tabard Inn joins the pilgrimage, some are certain it is not really for spiritual enrichment, but to get more business.

At Christmas we ought to be more charitable in our judgment of others, beginning with the inn-keeper.

*   *   *

A small mountain town had but two hotels. A traveller rode up, paused, and looked inquiringly about.
Traveller: 'Say, which of these two hotels is better?'

70

Town dweller: 'Stranger, no matter which one you go to, you'll wish you had gone to the other.'

During the preparations for the school nativity play, one young lad fell passionately in love with the little girl who had been cast as Mary. He was very keen to have the part of Joseph. But alas, this was not to be. He was chosen to play the inn-keeper. Come the day, with the hall full of parents and loved ones, Mary and Joseph knock on the door of the inn and ask for a room. 'You can come in Mary,' said the inn-keeper, 'but you buzz off Joseph.'

Saint What's Her Name?

She's in so many Christmas pageants I almost thought she was in the Bible – the inn-keeper's wife. Luke's account of the birth of Jesus is admittedly pretty sparse: 'And while they were there (in Bethlehem), the time came for her to be delivered. And she gave birth to her first born son and wrapped him in swaddling clothes, and laid him in a manger, because there was no place for them in the inn.' Maybe Mary and Joseph, in desperation, found the stable on their own. Maybe no one helped them at all.

But we like to think that the world isn't that cold, and that somebody – perhaps the inn-keeper's wife – cared enough to do something.

In my mind's eye I can see her rather clearly. She moves with an air of great authority – strong, efficient, knowing what to do. No doubt this night she is very busy with a full house of weary and disgruntled taxpayers. She is probably exhausted, with hurting feet and an aching back.

She may not be particularly religious, and certainly she is no mystic. She may well hope for the arrival of the Messiah, but doesn't just spend her days waiting. She is too busy.

She is accustomed to dealing with a wine-guzzling, rude public, and she may well be a tough, rough-talking 'broad', but she has genuine human sympathy for the young girl standing in front of her on the verge of labour, and the distraught young husband beside her. I can see her getting a lamp and some blankets and taking them to the stable. I see her tossing fresh straw and laying blankets over it, making the best she can of a desperate situation.

And I see her becoming a kind of spontaneous midwife. She probably has more experience with birth than either Mary or Joseph. Perhaps she wipes

Mary's brow and coaches her through the birth, cuts the umbilical cord, cleans and wraps the infant, and lays him in his mother's arms.

She smiles encouragingly and says she will look in a little later, and then rushes off to tend to the demands of other guests, not realising that she was the first ever to hold in her arms, Immanuel.

It's all apocryphal of course. There may never have been an inn-keeper's wife. But then, there might have been. There are people like that who simply do what they do, not because they have great insight into divine mysteries, but because they feel for the other person's plight, because they care.

Even in the Christmas pageant, the inn-keeper's wife isn't a starring role. It's just a walk on. She probably comes last on the billing and doesn't even have a name – just 'Inn-keeper's wife'. Not even 'Inn-keeper' – just 'Inn-keeper's wife'.

But I really like her.

I think I even love her – Saint What's-Her-Name.

Donn Crail.

The Baby Jesus

Baby Jesus. I wonder what he was like. I wonder if he caught colds and had colic, if he squirmed a lot and kicked the bedcovers off at night. I wonder if he smeared food all over his face. I wonder if he was like other babies. I hope so, I really do.

I hope Mary didn't treat him with awe. I hope she had the capacity to forget who he was – if she really knew – and to offer him the greatest gift of motherhood which, next to birth, is the telling of rules and the demand for their keeping. I hope he had to learn, and to learn in all the ways children must learn.

Do you suppose he went through the 'terrible twos'? Can it be that he used to cling to Mary's leg, and cry when she left him to go to the well. Did he resist sleep and feel sorry for himself when denied a treat?

If it seems irreverent to talk this way, if it seems to belittle the Saviour, then remember it is said of him that he was in every respect a man, as well as God in the flesh. No, what *is* crass and belittling is to deify his humanity. That is why I hope he caught colds and clung to his mother's leg and climbed trees.

I wonder if he walked early and talked in sentences by a year-and-a-half and could recite from the *Torah* at three. I hope not. Deliver me from precocious children, from the terrible infants who wear the attitudes of a *prima donna*. I hope he knew all about scraped noses and bruised knees.

I wonder what the baby Jesus was like. If he was like I hope he was, none of it would have subtracted one iota from his glory, which began with the most commonplace of all human actions, the action of birth. Thus the commonplace, the ordinary, the average, all in one baby, grew to become the very best of all answers to the greatest of all our needs, because God had become man.

Robert E Karsten.

When God wants an important thing done in this world or a wrong righted, he goes about it in a very singular way. He doesn't release his thunderbolts or stir up his earth-quakes. He simply has a tiny baby born, perhaps in a very humble home, perhaps of a very humble mother. And he puts the idea or purpose into the mother's heart. And she puts it in the baby's mind, and then – God waits. The great events of this world are not battles and elections and earth-quakes and thunderbolts. The great events are babies, for each child comes with the message that God is not yet discouraged with us, but is still expecting goodwill to become incarnate in each human life.

Edward McDonald.

73

The Baby Star
(A story for young children)

Flame was a baby star, but, like all stars, the more he grew, the brighter he became. Flame wasn't a very happy star, because he didn't have many friends, so he always took a great interest in what was going on down on earth. That kept him busy, because as the earth turned round ever so slowly, Flame could see different parts of it at different times.

This particular day, Flame was quite excited. The thing was, he had found some friends. Every night for a week now he had been watching some men riding camels across the desert, and every night they seemed to look straight up at him before they started on their way again. He could hardly wait to find out where they were going. So he waited and watched as, slowly, the world turned below. Suddenly Flame called out: 'Oh dear, it's cloudy!' Now you all know that when it's cloudy you can't see the stars, but did you ever think that when it's cloudy, the stars can't see us?

Flame thought for a long time. Then he decided that the only thing to do was to shine as brightly as he could, and point his rays straight down into the clouds. So he spun and spun and spun and spun, until he shone more brightly than he had ever done. And when he stopped, exhausted and very hot, he looked to see if he had managed to pierce the cloud with his light – and to his utter amazement he saw that the clouds had parted and his light was shining down onto a little town.

Quickly Flame looked around to see if he could see his friends – and there they were, just a few miles away! Flame was so pleased to see them, and felt all warm and happy when one of the men looked up and pointed towards him. Then Flame watched as the men gathered their things together, got on their camels and set off. Flame thought he'd have a look over the town as they were travelling, and saw lots of people coming and going in the streets. He heard a lot of noise coming from one building, but couldn't see what was going on inside.

But just then, one of the shafts of his light caught a space in the rafters of the shed outside. Flame peered through and, to his surprise, saw a baby sleeping in his mother's arms. Then Flame caught sight of his friends getting down from their camels, taking some shiny things from their saddle-bags, and going into the shed. Quickly Flame found the space in the rafters and peered through again. All his friends were laying down their shiny things among the hay.

74

Flame thought for a moment. This must be a very special baby indeed, for Flame's friends had travelled a very long way to give him these presents. Flame wished he were able to give the baby a present too, but he was so far away, and besides, he didn't have anything to give him. Then Flame saw that the baby had wakened up. Everyone there held up their shiny things for him to see, but he reached out his hand and caught a shaft of Flame's light, then he smiled and dropped back off to sleep.

Flame couldn't believe it, and for long nights after that he wondered why the baby had liked his light so much — after all, that was the only thing Flame knew how to do. But that's just it. Doing what we can do as well as we can, is all that is asked of any of us.

Jean Montgomerie.

The Wise Men

Many of our ideas about the Wise men are based on tradition rather than the account which Matthew gives us in his gospel. We talk for instance of there being 'three' wise men, when in fact the Bible does not say how many there were. This notion probably stems from the fact that they presented *three* gifts – gold, frankincense and myrrh – and the unwarranted conclusion that each gift must have been brought by a different person.

We also assume they were kings, for that is how they are depicted in classical paintings, and in carols such as 'We three kings of Orient are'. But again Matthew does not say anything about them being kings. What probably happened was that early Christian piety linked them with various old Testament texts, which spoke of kings coming from afar to Zion: 'Nations shall come to your light, and kings to the brightness of your rising.' (Isaiah 60, v. 3) 'May the kings of Tarshish and of the isles render him tribute, may the kings of Sheba and Seba bring gifts.' (Psalm 72, v.10).

An Armenian 'Gospel of the Infancy' which was written in the 5th century makes this equation. It even gives the kings names; Melchior, king of the Persians; Caspar, king of the Indians, and Balthasar, king of the Arabs. But in fact all that Matthew says is that they were 'from the East'.

The most widely held view is that the magi were part scientist, part astronomer, part astrologer. Their long journey to obscure Palestine had to do with a strange phenomenon in the sky and their interpretation of that phenomenon. It had also much to do with a star in their hearts and an irresistible calling to their souls that demanded attention. Even though they were clever men, they must have appeared as fools to their contemporaries for allowing the course of their lives to be so influenced by this urging in their souls.

The feast of the Epiphany which is celebrated on 6 January recalls how the Wise men came and knelt before the Christ child. The word Epiphany means 'manifestation' or 'coming to light'. Today we often use the word to describe some life-altering experience, or some insight gained in a loaded moment. In a moment of epiphany we exclaim, 'Aha! So that is it!'

*   *   *

Today many lay down their gold and frankincense and myrrh at other shrines and presumptuously present God with their 'cheese-parings and candle-ends'.

In reply to the teacher's question, one little boy informed her that the wise men brought 'Gold, frankincense and mirth'.

Three Other Wise Men

One Christmas Eve in San Quentin prison, almost as a gesture of sarcasm, the prisoners hung socks outside their cells. Unlike previous governors, the newly appointed governor responded. The prisoners' gesture seemed infinitely pathetic, so he despatched prison officers to purchase whatever fruit and chocolate they could get at that late hour. Shortly after midnight each sock was filled. Writing later of that incident, one of the prisoners Donald Lowrie said, 'This was the nearest thing to the Christ-Spirit that I saw at San Quentin.'

Johann Oberlin who lived in the 18th century was the Protestant minister of Waldach in the mountainous district of Alsace. One bitter December day while returning from a neighbouring village across the snow-covered mountains, he suddenly took ill. He knew he must press on for many had frozen to death through sitting down to rest. He had not gone far when he collapsed. On regaining consciousness he found himself in a little hut gazing up into the rugged face of a stranger who was giving him brandy. The stranger who had obviously carried him to the hut, stayed with him until he was stronger. Then he accompanied him to Waldach. Oberlin wanted to repay his kindness, but the man would take nothing. He would not even tell Oberlin his name. 'Pastor, when you tell me the Good Samaritan's name, I will tell you my name.'

I recall a man coming to my home in Glasgow and handing me a beautiful book. He explained that he had overheard a conversation in the local bookshop concerning a family where one of the boys was desperately keen to get this book for Christmas, but which his mother had admitted she could not afford. Anxious to remain anonymous, and to avoid the mother any embarrassment, he wondered if I would deliver the book.

'When you give, don't let your left hand know what your right hand is doing, so that giving may be in secret.' Jesus also said, 'Whoever hears these words of mine and acts upon them, I will liken unto a 'wise man'. The striking characteristic of these three wise men, the prison governor, the rugged man of the mountains and the Glaswegian, was their compassion, which expressed itself in doing good secretly. Lloyd Douglas was right to describe such anonymous giving as a 'magnificent obsession'.

Celebrating Love

GOD'S LOVE
'The love for equals is a human thing – of friend for friend, brother for brother. It is to love what is loving and lovely. The world smiles. The love for those less fortunate is a beautiful thing – the love for those who suffer, for those who are poor, the sick, the failures, the unlovely. This is compassion, and it touches the heart of the world. The love for the more fortunate is a rare thing – to love those who succeed where we fail, to rejoice without envy with those who rejoice, the love of the poor for the rich, of the black man for the white man. The world is always bewildered by its saints. And then there is the love for the enemy – love for the one who does not love you, but mocks, threatens and inflicts pain. This is God's love.'

F Buechner.

DEMONSTRATING LOVE
Love will find a way; indifference an excuse.
The Christmas season reminds us that demonstrating love is better than defining it. So let us remember at Christmas those who find enjoyment hardest to come by, the unpublicised poor, the recently bereaved, the sick and the anxious, above all the lonely, especially those who keep secret the real depth of their loneliness.

GOD MOMENTS

Love is the reason why suddenly at Christmas, for no apparent reason we find our eyes misting over. We see a candle burning in a church, or hear a brass band playing a carol. We see a child fast asleep with his arm clutched round a stuffed animal, or see coloured lights blinking in the window of a remote farm-house. The tear in the eye is often the result of love at work in us. Note these moments when tears come to your eyes for they are often God-moments.

GOOD OLD HUMANS

As I see the crowds thronging the busy thoroughfares of our city loaded down with parcels and bulging plastic bags, I keep wondering about the destination of all these goodies they have just bought. I am sure the vast bulk of their festal bundles are for others – the children, the family, friends, sweethearts – and I feel like shouting, 'Good old Humans, there is a lot of love in you if only you'd show it more often.' Think of the millions of pounds donated to the Children in Need Fund, and the generosity shown to Radio Clyde's Cash for Kids project, or the hundreds of schoolchildren collecting for Yorkhill Children's Hospital, not to mention the long list of friendly, loving things done for the elderly and the sick and housebound. Above all there's a strong atmosphere of kindness and goodwill around 25 December. Could this be a gift from God to our weary world?

God keeps stirring up a lot of love in us for others. so when you're handing over your gift or gratefully receiving one, or even when it's only a handshake of greeting, or a Christmas smile, God is there, whether you are aware of it or not.

Thomas Winning, R.C. Archbishop of Glasgow,
writing in the *Glasgow Herald*.

DEATHLESS LOVE

She was a quiet little old lady in an eventide home, all alone without relatives. She was a rather pathetic figure at Christmas time until a package came addressed to her. 'He never forgot me,' she exclaimed, opening the package as pleased as a child, and showing us an expensive handbag and a corsage of red roses. The card was signed by her husband long dead. He had arranged with a trustee to select a gift and flowers to be sent to her from him each Christmas.

*   *   *

A few days before Christmas the following advert appeared in a local newspaper. 'A loving kitten desires position as companion to small child.

79

Will also do light mouse work.'

Puppy love can sometimes be the prelude to a dog's life.

An Audrey Drain recalls how as a small child at Sunday School she learned several hymns including 'Jesus Loves Me'. But her version went, 'Little ones to him belong. They are weak but tea is strong.'

Children were asked, 'What is love?' One girl replied, 'Love is when the person reading you a bedtime story doesn't skip any of the pages.'

Dear Minister, I know that God loves everyone, but he has never met my sister. Yours sincerely, Peter (aged 7).

All the world loves a lover – except those who are waiting to use the phone.

For Christmas one husband gave his wife a heart-shaped snow shovel!

A hug is a perfect Christmas gift. One size fits all, and nobody minds if you exchange it.

The best exercise for the heart is to reach down and help people up.

This will be a better world when the power of love replaces the love of power.

God and Santa

The poem ''Twas the night before Christmas' was written by a professor at a New York Theological Seminary. Clement Moore was in no danger of confusing poetic fantasy with religious truth, or a seasonal Santa with a constant Christ. His poem was intended to provide only 'a good, honest, hearty laugh'. He had no intention of exploiting the credulity of the very young, or establishing a Santa cult. But he was aware that 'pretend people' can add excitement to childhood. They can help cultivate a child's imagination. Psychological damage is only done to children if parents fraudulently insist that magical creatures such as Santa Claus and Peter Pan be accepted as flesh and blood people. For Clement Moore 'St Nick' was a symbol of caring and sharing, certainly not to be confused with God from whom all blessings flow.
When children are old enough to raise questions about Santa coming down chimneys or storks bringing babies, or fairies trading money for teeth, they

deserve straight answers. If parents continue to be devious in responding to these questions, the children will go elsewhere for reliable information, and problems of trust could well arise. But if children are taught early on to separate figments of the imagination from abiding reality, such imaginary creatures as Santa, far from leading to disillusionment, can enrich childhood.

Although Christmas is a festival which celebrates kindness and goodwill, it can unfortunately introduce children at an early age to the injustices and inequalities of the world. Many poorer children resent the fact that so often the toys of their dreams end up in the homes of better off children.

A Londoner, recalling her childhood, tells how one particular year she wanted a doll and a pram from Santa. Her mother warned her that Santa might not be able to give her both, but she was sure he would do what he could. When she opened her stocking she found four new pennies, a few nuts, a tangerine, an apple, a comic and a rag doll perched on top. She was pleased with it until she went out to play. Her friend emerged from her house with a beautiful twin pram and twin dolls. Later that day she said to her mother, 'Father Christmas is not very fair Mum, is he?'

*　　*　　*

'When we were very young we had to pen in our best writing a courteous letter to Santa, craving the gift we most desired. That year I clearly wanted a box of paints, although my artistic efforts were pitiful. They still are. Very small and struggling with the intricacies of English spelling, I asked Santa for a box of 'pants', hoping he would be 'grashus' enough to give me such a gift. My jeering brother Bill told me too late about my spelling errors. He appeared in my bedroom next day at dawn to discover what I had received. He was radiant because he had been given a Meccano set and an electric motor. At the foot of my small bed I saw the usual bulging stocking and a parcel. 'You've got your *pants* all right, Dopey,' he grinned. And I had. They were stuffed into the top of my stocking. Navy blue! I lifted my voice and decided not to be consoled. Santa had taken me too literally. Then my brother who did not suffer tears, ripped open the parcel beside my stocking. It contained books and the coveted paint box!

Meta Wright, Dornoch.

William French tells how an American regiment threw a Christmas party for some Japanese kids. The programme featured the youngsters singing 'Silent Night' in English, and a soldier in a red Santa Claus costume and cotton whiskers giving out presents. It was a really friendly, happy party, with lots of food and parcels for everybody. 'Then a little eight-year-old asked a question. Roughly translated it was: "Whose birthday is it? The man with the whiskers?" Someone told him we were celebrating our Saviour's birthday. But he was confused. From all he could see, Santa was the main attraction.'

Whose birthday is it? Do the millions of pounds of Christmas advertising tell us? Or the lavish displays in shop windows, the elaborate decorations, the light strung trees? Santa Claus is everywhere – but even the children might get more out of Christmas if they knew about Him whose birthday it is.

*   *   *

Writing in *The Observer*, the magazine of the United Church of Canada, a Terry Shillington expressed his reservations about Santa Claus.
'It's true that our churches bulge at Christmas time. It's true that songs of Jesus' birth ring out, and exhortations to peace and love are everywhere. And even though our Christmas cards and house decorations favour the jolly figure of Santa Claus, still Christmas is really about Jesus – we say. But our children know better. As in most matters, they are quick to perceive what we really believe.

Last year during Advent, one of our Sunday school teachers asked a pre-school class who had made the sun, moon and stars. The answer came back, 'Santa Claus'. A few years ago I carelessly began some Sunday morning remarks to the boys and girls by asking them who came at Christmas. The answer of course, 'Santa Claus'. Accordingly, some parents try to keep Santa in the background. But he won't stay there. He elbows his way to the front, with his sack of toys, and for the young, occupies centre stage.

Still what could be wrong with letting Santa enjoy the limelight for a few years of a child's life? Isn't it all harmless fun? But Santa's popularity rests on the material possessions that he promises, the bulging stocking, the sleigh heaped high with toys. Children wait anxiously for what they will get, and getting is the theme. One sensitive parent, commenting on the selfish 'What's for me?' attitude that Santa causes in his children, erupted last winter, 'I just hate my kids for about a month around Christmas.'

This preoccupation with getting things, into which Santa initiates our young, is a life-style we can no longer afford. More and more we are learning that we simply cannot go on producing more, consuming more and throwing out more garbage. As *we* catalogue our social crises, we can trace many of them back to a way of life which exalts things above persons. In Santa, are we imparting the values we really want to encourage?

What can we do? We can tell our family the story of Jesus. That means more than a trip to church on Christmas Eve. The family needs to experience Jesus' coming with as much colour and drama as we have used to celebrate Santa. My wife and I build a nativity scene in our living room each Christmas, with figures four or five feet high and a huge stable made of cardboard. Each December the family makes a trip to a farm to get the straw and then assembles the scene together. Our children begin asking months in advance, 'When will we build the manger scene?'.

It is possible to choose a style of celebration which does not stress giving expensive gifts at all. The custom of affluent people exchanging gifts which few truly need, has little to do with Jesus's birth either. We can begin to find ways of celebration which stress enjoying family and friends, not getting things. This might include making our own modest gifts for loved ones and giving our money to a place of real need.

Can we continue leading our young into a celebration of Christmas which stresses an over-weight, over-age, over-priced myth and the things he will bring? Surely both the times and the gospel make it imperative to teach our children radically different values.'

More Blessed to Give

A Mr Morrison tells how one cold blustery Christmas Eve, he left his office early. Turning up his coat collar he hastened to where his car was parked. It was however some time before he got there, for in a shop doorway he spotted a little boy, standing shivering. Noticing that he had been crying, Mr Morrison stopped and asked what was the matter. The boy answered, 'Nothing mister. I'm O.K.' Mr Morrison smiled and said, 'Sonny you are not all right. Something is upsetting you. Tell me what it is and I might be able to help you. The little lad then explained how his father had given him a ten pound note to go and get cigarettes and some groceries. 'The ten pounds must have slipped out of my hand, and I'm afraid to go back home.' 'But you can't stay here. You will freeze to death. On you go home. I am sure your Dad will understand.' But the boy shook his head. 'You don't know my Dad. He's been drinking and he'll kill me.'
Mr Morrison took the little lad into the shop and bought the cigarettes and groceries. The bill came to eight pounds. He gave the lad the £2 change and told him not to tell his father what had happened. He also expressed the hope that he would have a happy Christmas. Thanking Mr Morrison profusely, he set off with his purchases. He had not gone far when he turned around, ran back, put his arms round Mr Morrison and with his voice choked up said, 'I wish you were my Dad.'
Relating the incident later Mr Morrison told how he was tempted to look and see if he could find another boy who had lost money!

*   *   *

With my mind I do believe
'Tis more blessed to give than to receive
And yet at Christmas I secretly fret
When I send more cards than I ever get.

Things of the spirit differ from things material in that the more you give, the more you have. The comedian has an immensely better time than the audience. To modernise the adage, to give is more fun than to receive, especially if you have wit enough to give to those who don't expect it. Surprise is the most primitive joy of humanity. Surprise is the first reason for a baby's laughter. And at Christmas time when we are all a little childish I hope, surprise is the flavour of our keenest joys. We all remember the thrill with which we once heard, behind some closed door, the rustle and crackle of paper parcels being tied up. We knew that we were going to be surprised.

Christopher Morley.

The Dutch author Jaap ter Haar in his book *Boris* tells how during the siege of Leningrad by the Germans, the city was reduced to rubble and the people were ravaged by hunger. Young Boris went to a Christmas play with hopes that food might be served. When it was, Boris instead of eating himself, selflessly stuck his bread and slice of meat into a piece of paper and smuggled it home. He then carefully prepared the meat for his mother. A seemingly humble gift, yet under the circumstances, a gift representative of life itself. Even though his mother would have preferred that Boris would have the meat and bread, she accepted it because she knew that 'in this life there are some gifts that cannot be refused.'

The Family

'Father McGlinchey, don't you miss the joys of family life at Christmas?'

A FAMILY IS A PLACE
to cry
and laugh
and vent frustration
to ask for help
and tease
and yell
to be touched and hugged
and smiled at.

A FAMILY IS PEOPLE
who care when you are sad
who love you no matter what
who share your triumphs
who don't expect you to be perfect
just growing with honesty
in your own direction

A FAMILY IS A CIRCLE
where we learn to like ourselves
where we learn to make good decisions
where we learn to think before we do
where we learn integrity and
table manners and respect for
other people
where we are special
where we share ideas
where we listen and are listened to
where we learn the rules of life
to prepare ourselves for the world.

THE WORLD IS A PLACE
where anything can happen.
If we grow up in a loving family
we are ready for the world.

Bethlehem and Nazareth

A friend tells of conducting an Advent service in Bettyhill, a Highland village on the north coast of Scotland. He began his talk to the children by asking where Jesus was born. To his surprise there was no response. Trying to be helpful, he told them the place began with the letters B-E-T. Only then did a seven-year-old tentatively ask, 'Was it Bettyhill?'

Bethlehem was probably not all that different in appearance from Bettyhill. Equally insignificant was the village of Nazareth where Jesus spent his boyhood. It was in fact such a small drab outpost of the Roman Empire that Nathaniel just could not believe that God could bring healing to the nations out of such a backwater. 'Can anything good come out of Nazareth?' he asked. Nathaniel's doubts were heightened by the fact that he came from Cana, another small Galilean town. Such jealously and rivalry between small towns still exists.

Yet it was from Nazareth that there came forth a Man who divided history into Before and After, a Jew who was so much a citizen of the world that most people do not think of Him as a Jew. Though born and raised in an obscure village, he was inspired by a view of life and a purpose that embraced the whole of humanity. It was in Nazareth that the world's most significant thinking was done. His words clung to people's memories by their rightness and brightness, their simplicity and profundity. For Jesus the secret of life was love – not love as passion or liking, but love as caring, as a creative, healing force in the world. The final verdict on his life was that if ever God revealed himself to the world, if ever heaven appeared on earth, it was in the Person and work of Jesus of Nazareth.

The title Jesus of Nazareth reminds us that what really matters is not where a person comes from, but the faith and ideals that motivate that person. Biographical dictionaries remind us that little villages have their fair share of distinguished sons and daughters. In every small town there are people who have small and mean thoughts, but let us not forget, that is not an inevitable consequence of living in small places. Out of the village of Epworth in Lincolnshire came a man who changed the course of British history. Out of a Bedford jail and from a thatched roof cottage in Ayr came great classics of British literature. Out of an American log cabin came one of the most influential Americans of the 19th century. As John Wesley, John Bunyan, Robert Burns and Abraham Lincoln remind us, all important is the quality of the thinking that goes on within the people who live and work there.

Can any good thing come out of Nazareth or Bettyhill or . . . The answer is YES provided the ideas and the thinking and the compassion that motivate us are big enough.

Missing What is Important

If someone had said to the Roman Emperor Augustus that first Christmas Eve, 'Look here Augustus, leave what you are doing alone. What really matters tonight is the fact that a peasant woman has had a baby in Bethlehem.' Augustus would probably have concluded the person was mentally unbalanced.

In the time of Augustus, powerful Roman armies tramped over the greater part of the known world. Roman officials were certain they knew the future course of history. The Empire would go from strength to strength until all hostile tribes were crushed, and the Emperor would reign supreme.

How different it turned out. Not the Roman legions, but a Jewish carpenter quietly determined the future that was to be. Not the Emperor who ruthlessly destroyed his enemies, but a wandering teacher who forgave them and became the central character of the centuries.

Those grand occasions which send news hungry reporters and cameramen hurrying from all airts, that make the news vendors yell their heads off, are seldom the events that change the course of history. A distinguished journalist, Malcolm Muggeridge, put it thus: 'I have observed a strange thing over many years in this business of news gathering and news presentation. By some infallible process media people always manage to miss the most important thing. . . . In moments of humility I realise that if I had been correspondent to the Holy Land at the time of our Lord's ministry, I should almost certainly have spent my time knocking about the entourage of Pontius Pilate, finding out what the Jewish hierarchy was up to, or lurking around King Herod's court with the hope of signing up Salome to write her exclusive memoirs.'

Christmas reminds us that we will be woefully misled if we evaluate life by size or noise or pomp.

No Peace on Earth

In his poem 'The morning of Christ's Nativity', John Milton pictures that first Christmas in words of great beauty:

> No war or battle's sound
> Was heard the world around;
> The idle spear and shield were high uphung
> The hooked chariot stood
> Unstained with hostile blood;
> (The trumpet spake not to the armed throng
> And kings sat with awful eye
> As if they surely knew their sovereign Lord was by)
> But peaceful was the night
> Wherein the Prince of Light
> His reign of peace upon the earth began.

It is beautiful poetry. But it falsifies the grim realities of that first Christmas. There was no special quietness about the night. Bethlehem was no lost Eden where everything was idyllic and perfect. The world went on its way as usual, quite unaware of what was happening in the stable at Bethlehem. Bethlehem must have been a noisy place that night, for in it had gathered a great crowd of travellers – all brought together on an unpopular errand a Roman census.

Matthew's story of the birth of Jesus has a different feel from Luke's. Whereas Luke tells his story in pastoral rustic tones, Matthew tells his story against the background of deception and brutality, of human folly and selfishness, of plottings and killings. The slaughter of the infants in Bethlehem was in keeping with Herod. The year before, he had killed three of his own sons. Earlier he had killed their mother as part of a general slaughter of his in-laws. Shortly after the Bethlehem massacre he rounded up many of the leading citizens of Judea, locked them in the Circus at Jericho, and gave orders that they should be killed when he died. Aware that he was seriously ill, this was his one way of guaranteeing there would be mourning when he died. He knew few if any would shed tears at his passing.

Jesus was born in rough tough surroundings like two thirds of our fellow human beings in the Third World. He was hurried away by his parents from a scene of slaughter, like many babies today. He was one of a refugee family, like the millions of displaced people still putting the 20th century to shame. He was not a white man, but a brown-skinned Palestinian Jew. He was coloured like the majority of the world's population.

The background to the modern Christmas is little different from the original Christmas – hatred, war, poverty, homelessness, famine and death. A Christmas poem by Longfellow reflects the modern situation more accurately:

> I heard the bells on Christmas day
> Their old familiar carols play
> And wild and sweet the words repeat
> Of peace on earth, good will to men.
> And in despair I bowed my head:
> 'There is no peace on earth' I said,
> 'For hate is strong, and mocks the song
> Of peace on earth, goodwill to men.'

What a tragedy that we have wrapped the birth of Jesus in the swaddling clothes of sentimentality, that we have divorced the Christ story from the hard world of reality, for it is the one thing which can help us find meaning, purpose, comfort, inner strength, faith and hope in the darkness of so much that has gone so terribly wrong.

The shepherds and wise men, living as they did in an ugly and unjust world, might well have cried in despair, 'Look what the world has come to!' Instead they looked at the babe asleep in the stable and cried, 'Look what has come to the world.'

*   *   *

Christmas carollers sing about peace on earth, but they don't tell us where!

> Hark the Herald Angels sing
> But we cannot hear a thing
> Just the sleek jet bomber's whistle
> And the roar of guided missile.
> Fearful all ye nations cringe
> Mankind's on the damnest binge;
> Sing your songs of fear and hate
> You may not have long to wait.
>
> Anon.

A carved nativity scene brought to Madrid from South America was worth its weight in gold. The figures, animals and the stable, had been carved out of pure cocaine worth £2 million.

A little boy was watching a western on T.V. His mother was known for her strong convictions against drinking. She came into the room just as the T.V. hero was on his way into a saloon. The little boy said, 'Don't worry Mum, he isn't going to drink anything. He's just going in to kill a man.'

Lady Sarah Hussey tells how Joyce Grenfell was once baby-sitting for her niece and nephew, Sally and Lang. She had read Sally a bed-time story. When she finally went through to see Lang, she found him fast asleep. But lying on his bedside table she noticed a little note which he had scribbled, 'Remember to hit Sally in the morning.'

A Glasgow minister tells of once conducting a Christmas day broadcast. He knew that two of his aunts would be listening, sisters who because of a difference of opinion earlier that year, no longer spoke. At the end of his Christmas message which was on the theme of reconciliation, he suggested that if any of his radio audience had become estranged from a relative or former friend, they should at the end of the broadcast contact that person and thus make Christmas day once again a time of peace and goodwill. Later that day one of his aunts phoned to say how much she had enjoyed the broadcast. Then she added, 'When the broadcast was over I went and sat by the phone, but my sister didn't call.'

91

Had I Been Around

If I had been around that first Christmas I am convinced that I would have seen and heard Nothing.

I would have been so busy cleaning the living room, or worrying about deductions and how not to pay the capital gains tax, that I would not even have looked up to see any stars, let alone that special one that suddenly was there where no star had ever been before.

I would have been so uneasy about the state of the world, so anxious about where I was going to live and what I was going to do tomorrow, so frightened by a sense of chaos and a nagging suspicion that life means nothing at all, that I would not even have heard a whole massed group of choirs and orchestras playing and singing fortissimo 'Glory to God in the highest and, on earth, Peace, good will to men', let alone one solitary angel voice saying quietly and firmly: 'Do not be afraid.'

I'd have been so rooted to the spot, so surrounded by habit, so fixed in what I knew that I knew, I could not even have run down from the nearby hills, let alone embarked upon a long and dangerous journey across miles and miles of trackless desert, where all there was to see (I'd have been sure) was just another squawling baby, like any other new-born squawling little baby whose mother and father were nobodies from a nothing little town somewhere out across the hills. Yes if I'd been around and been me on that first Christmas, the whole thing would have gone right past me, I'm positive. So lucky for me that, being me, I'm here now.

Because, even if it took almost two thousand years, I do believe it may be finally happening to me. I do believe that, finally, I may be on the verge of seeing and hearing it all myself. Oh, I hope so. I do hope so. Because, from what I hear from others who have seen and heard, I know I wouldn't want to miss it for the world.

Elizabeth Berryhill.

Some of us think, 'If I had only been there! How quick I would have been to help the Baby. I would have washed his linen . . . ' We say that because we know how great Christ is, but if we had been there at that time we would have done no better than the people of Bethlehem. . . . Why don't we do it now? We have Christ in our neighbour.

Martin Luther.

Coming and Going

A verb that counts a great deal today is the verb to 'go'. A man is judged by the amount of 'go' he has in him. 'Keep going' is our basic philosophy. Nothing has so far hindered for long the onward march of mankind. When he came to a broad river, he made a bridge; on the shores of the ocean he built great ships; and confronted by the abyss of space he launched a lunar capsule. The sky is no longer the limit.

But when we come to cross the threshold of the infinite, and seek to probe the mystery of the eternal God, then we are as little children. We can only wait and wonder, helpless before a dimension denied to us. If we are to know God then God himself must come to us. There can be no other way. There must be an Advent.

It is this Advent of faith which underlies the strange joy of Christmas time. The first glimpse of glory came to the shepherds amid the dark fields of Bethlehem. Now the song encircles the earth and unites the hearts of millions in an undying hope. 'For unto you is born this day in the City of David a Saviour which is Christ the Lord.'

It is in this human life, as the J B Phillips translation puts it, 'that God gives a full and complete expression of Himself within the physical limits that He has set.'

Can such things be? Is it possible that in this child dwelt the sublime and eternal presence of the living God? That in Him was the secret of life and the mystery of death? The seed of a new world? The glory of unconquerable love? The hope of generations unborn?

The mind staggers. But the deep places of the heart recognise the truth which the reason cannot grasp, and cries out for joy, 'Amen! His name is Immanuel – God is with us!'

Life, we often say casually is just a coming and a going. Perhaps we are nearer the heart of the matter than we ever realised. We have, indeed, far to go, and none of us can see what lies beyond tomorrow in our going.

But the Christian knows also the secret of the Coming. The One who came to us; who shared our mortal life; who loved us to the uttermost; and now abides with us for ever.

Nelson Gray, *Glasgow Evening Citizen.*

Along the pathways to the stars
We toil towards Jupiter and Mars.
Good God! It seems we have lost our mind,
In leaving Bethlehem behind.

No Forwarding Address

A weary traveller arrived at the hotel in Bethlehem and checked in. As he signed the hotel register, he said to the sleepy desk clerk, 'Say! I hear you had some excitement here a few weeks ago.'
The sleepy desk clerk replied, 'Not much of a story really. Some time during the night a squalling kid was born in the stable. Some shepherds, smelling of sheep dip, came in from the hills and had a look at the kid. Later on three well-dressed men came into town from the eastern throughway. They left some expensive gifts with the parents. And that's about all there is, except that a few days later the husband and wife disappeared suddenly. Nobody knew where they had gone. Anyhow when you're bunking in a stable nobody bothers to ask for a forwarding address.'

*   *   *

An infant school teacher told the children the story of the flight of Mary and Joseph into Egypt with Jesus. She then asked the class to draw the scene. One boy drew Joseph leading his donkey, with Mary riding on it holding the baby Jesus. Behind the tiny procession walked a little servant boy carrying a suitcase on which were the initials 'J.C.'

Parents have to decide whether to have a puppy and have the house messed up, or children and have their lives messed up.

Christmas Dreams

We are told 'An angel of the Lord appeared to Joseph in a dream.' Dreams had an important place in that first Christmas. A dream turned the Wise Men homeward another way. Because of a dream the holy family fled Judea. It was a time of dreams.

Nor has man stopped dreaming at Christmas. Clement Moore in *The Night Before Christmas* has his children tucked into their beds dreaming of sugar plums. Scrooge dreamed of Christmas Past, Present and Future. Irving Berlin dreamed of a 'White Christmas'. Henry Van Dyke dreamed his immortal story of 'The Other Wise Man'.

Christmas is still a dream time. It was so when you were little – with all the new toys. But now you are grown up what are your Christmas dreams?

Are you dreaming:
— of a New World that 'ain't gonna war no more'?
— of a Country, 'beautiful for patriot dreams'?
— of a Church, anchoring souls in life's stormy waters?
— of Friends, staunch in the give and take of life?
— of Loved Ones, ever committing their way to Christ's way?
— of a Better YOU, (the potential here, unlimited)?
Yes, what are your Christmas dreams? And are they God's

                                        From *These Days*.

God Was There

When Jesus was born,
There was no priest or pastor there,
No choir,
   No incense,
      No altar,
And no congregation.
But God was there –
And a cow or two
And sheep
And perhaps a donkey
And certainly a woman and a man.

This baby that was born there,
Like other babies,
Moved from the comfortable security of his mother's womb
Into an unsafe world
Where there was not only milk and love
But also bruising stones
And crosses
And hatred.
When he was a boy –
like other boys –
He played games
And carried water
And watched camel caravans
Without knowing whence they came
Or whither they went
But wondering.

And when he was a man –
like other men –
He got callouses on his hands
And blisters
And developed ideas
And convictions
For which he could die –
And for which he did die.

These things did not happen
In a church
Or a monastery
Or an ivory tower
But in villages,
Among people
On the highways and byways
Of this very world

Alexander T Coyle.

A Real Baby in the Manger

Father Keane was a priest in the Greenock area. Every Christmas, he set up a Nativity scene in the Chapel with life-sized figures.
Around the manger were grouped Mary and Joseph, the shepherds, the angels, even the sheep and a donkey. In the manger was a doll representing Jesus.
It was one of the highlights of the priest's year.
One particular Christmas, the priest had excitedly gone into the darkened Chapel to switch on the lights. He heard a baby crying and, strangely, it seemed to be coming from the manger. He tiptoed forward and, to his wonder, there was a real baby, instead of a doll, lying in the manger. Father Keane bent forward and gently lifted up the child.
As he did so, he caught sight of a little girl standing in the shadows and all at once he understood. For in her arms she was cradling the doll-like figure of the baby Jesus, and there was a look of infinite tenderness on her face. As the priest crossed over to her, she looked up and tears welled into her eyes. 'Father,' she said, apologetically, 'I just wanted to hold the baby Jesus, so I laid my wee brother in the manger so it wouldn't be empty.'
Father Keane swallowed hard – for, wonderful as his manger scene had been before, this simple act of a child had transformed it into a truly rich experience.

The Baby and the Man

In my study I have a book entitled *Lighten our Darkness*. Although I have on several occasions started to read it, I have never got beyond the second chapter. The problem is that to make sense of the whole, I have to start each time at page one. I am now familiar with the first few pages, but know nothing of the contents of the rest of the book. Likewise there are many who know almost word perfect the second chapter of Luke's Gospel. 'In those days there went out a decree from Caesar Augustus . . .' but they have never got much further with the story.

The emphasis put on the birth of Jesus and the baby Jesus is understandable. Take a baby anywhere and it steals the show. How proudly parents and grandparents tell of the first tooth, the first word, the first step. But a baby which remained a baby forever would be a pathetic figure. In Scotland, one month after we celebrate the birth of Jesus, we celebrate the birth of our national poet Robert Burns. Never once at a Burns' night have I heard any speaker extol Burns the baby, Burns asleep in his cot. Those who propose the 'Immortal Memory' speak rather of what he said and did as an adult, and the challenge he presented to his contemporaries.

A modern carol poses the valid question, 'Who else on his birthday is put back in his crib?' At Christmas we carol the infant king, but for many that is where the story ends. They forget that the baby Jesus is important only because of the person he became, and what he said and did. What a challenge he presented to that cruel, harsh, first century world, the challenge to create a new world founded on compassion and brotherhood, to serve rather than dominate, to be humble rather than proud, to forgive rather than take revenge. What a challenge he still presents to many of our rigid attitudes and prejudices. We are here, he said, to love God and care for one another. We impoverish ourselves when we forget the errand.

*   *   *

Bishop Fulton Sheen was one of America's outstanding communicators. Once at an end of the year T.V. award ceremony, he was nominated for the best religious broadcaster of the year. In his short speech of acceptance, he said, 'I feel it is time that I now also pay tribute to my four writers – Matthew, Mark, Luke and John.'

A teacher recalls showing her class a picture of Jesus riding into Jerusalem on that first Palm Sunday. As she did so a little voice from the back of the class was heard to say, 'Hasn't he grown a lot since Christmas?'

Come On All Ye Faithful

Shortly after his first grandchild was born, President Sadat flew from Cairo to Jerusalem to meet with the Israeli Prime Minister, Golda Meir. In her words of welcome, Golda Meir said to President Sadat, 'I have been a grandmother for some years. Let me give you a gift for your grandchild.' Sadat's chin trembled as he accepted the gift.

As I watched that historic meeting on television it struck me that peace on earth might be a real possibility, if only the leaders of the world's many warring factions were really to care for the future well-being of each others' grandchildren.

This conviction was reinforced by a story of a man who all his life had worked as a labourer. He once confided to his minister that he had never learned to read or write. 'Would you like to?' said the minister. 'I thought about it once,' the man said, but I never went to the first meeting. It is so embarrassing when you are forty-seven. I have got a reasonably well-paid job, a good family, a sense of humour, and earlier this year our daughter presented us with a wonderful little grand-daughter. So in many ways, although I cannot read, I am not too badly off.' 'But,' said the minister, 'would you not like one day to be able to read stories to your grand-daughter?' 'Well you have got me there,' said the man. 'I suppose I would.' His love for his grand-daughter and his desire to enrich her life finally prompted him to attend reading classes. For her sake he was willing to change, willing even to suffer embarrassment.

A recent Christmas drink driving advert highlighted the disastrous effects drink-driving can have on someone's grandchild. The advert said in effect, 'For the sake of someone's grandchild please don't drink and drive.' When I think of all the pain and brokenness that there is in the world brought about by human greed, spite and prejudice – broken hearts, broken homes, divided communities and nations, there are many other habits which I wish we would change for the sake of our grandchildren. The caring, forgiving, life-style advocated and exemplified by Jesus of Nazareth, is a far nobler one than our superficial, self-centred life-style, but alas many of us are too set in our ways or too embarrassed to change.

An unusual Christmas card portrayed a choir boy singing with might and main. The card was traditional enough, but the caption was different. What the small boy was represented as singing you will find in no hymn-book. 'O come on all ye faithful.' For the sake of our children and grandchildren let us resolve that our homes will be unashamedly Christian – not goody-goody, narrow-minded and intolerant of others' views – but lit up by the joyful and life-enriching faith of Him who was not only the Prince of Peace, but the Prince of Life.

Living Pictures

A twelve-year-old boy was heard to exclaim in disgust, 'Why must every book and film have a love story running through it?' For this lad the word 'love' meant almost nothing. Five years later, it was very different. In the interval a charming girl had captivated him. Her eyes and smile spoke volumes. He had fallen deeply in love. The word 'love' now meant a great deal. It had become a human being.

So it is with many abstract words. They mean little until they are incarnated in a human life. Words like goodness, graciousness and courage have their limitations. It is difficult to define such qualities in terms which don't themselves need defining. If asked to explain what I mean when I use these words, I would point to certain people whose lives portray these qualities. That I would say is what I mean by goodness or graciousness.

My wife and I once had a fascinating discussion with three other couples on what we meant by femininity. We really got into deep water. We finished up as far away from an exact definition as when we started, but we were all agreed concerning certain members of the female sex who had this indefinable quality.

Most abstract words are like this. They are not fully understood until for us they become flesh. Seeking to define faith for his readers, the writer of the letter to the Hebrews finally does so by pointing to people of great faith, men like Abraham and Moses. The word God is no exception. Without further definition the word is meaningless. Abstract definitions of God like the 'Idea of Perfection', the 'Ground of Being', the 'Principle of Concretion', convey little to the ordinary person of what God is really like. These very definitions need redefining.

A London social worker once said, 'When God started to write a creed for us, He did it, not in words that might change their meaning. He set before us a life.' In the fullness of time God chose to reveal himself in human terms, which are after all the terms we best understand. Despite our boasted intellectual prowess, God knows we need living pictures, more than abstractions. And so he gave us Jesus. In the introduction to his Gospel John says, 'The word became a human being, and full of truth and grace lived among us.'

It is a great pity that the earliest images of God which many were given are decidedly negative. God is the great kill-joy, a task-master and grim book-keeper, the one to whom one finally surrenders and thereafter lives a life of drabness and sacrifice. Others were brought up to believe that the love of God had to be earned. But because of Jesus' coming into the world, we no longer think of God thus. Jesus' concern was to enlarge life, to make it a more joyful thing. In Jesus, holding out hands of help and healing, befriending those who had no friends, forgiving those who sincerely sought forgiveness, enriching people's lives, we glimpse the nature of God.

Jesus did not come to establish another religion. He came to reveal the reality behind the appearance of things. Speaking of the change Jesus brought about in people's thinking about God who created and rules this universe, Joseph Newton said, 'For the first time people were glad about God.'

Backstairs at Bethlehem

Someone once said with tongue in cheek that the perfect marriage would be between a blind wife and a deaf husband! Whether such a partnership would be as perfect as imagined is doubtful, but I certainly never cease to marvel at how often marriage is a union between two people, one of whom is at his brightest in the morning, and one who just wants to be left alone until mid-morning – between one who likes to squeeze the toothpaste and one who prefers to roll it. How often marriage is a strange alliance between a man who refuses to believe there is a leak in the water-pipe, and a woman who is convinced she is about to drown – between one partner who likes to sleep with the windows shut, and one who likes to sleep with them wide-open, even in winter.

My wife being a fresh-air fanatic, our bedroom and bathroom windows are regularly open to allow the sea breezes to blow in. Inevitably from time to time a bird gets in as well! I vividly recall one such little feathered creature. We tried opening more windows, but to no avail. We tried 'shooing' it out, but it simply became more frightened. Finally I had to corner it, grip it firmly and carry it to the open window. The panic of the bird was obvious, its heart pumping furiously, its eyes almost popping out of their sockets.

Our feathered friend unfortunately did not understand we were kindly disposed to him. We wanted to release him from unnatural confines and give him back the freedom he was meant to enjoy. I don't know how I could have convinced the little creature of that, unless somehow I could have become a bird myself, and communicated in bird language the fact that I was not someone to be feared, that I was his friend.

Was it similar with God? Was that why he crept down the backstairs at Bethlehem?

Immortal Longings

A Scottish minister once told how away in the ranches of America there were rough men who were cradled in the glens and crofts of Scotland. 'You might live with them for months and years, and never know that they remembered home. Only some evening there would come a strain of music, some song, some pibroch, some Highland lilt and on that restless company there would fall a quietness. Then it took no prophet to discover that the thirst for the homeland was not dead.'

So it is I believe with our longing for God and goodness. They can be forgotten, but not easily eradicated. D H Lawrence said of his debased father, 'He forgot the God in him.' Though we too may forget God for a time and wander far from the paths of righteousness, it is doubtful if we ever fully lose the awareness that there is something in our natures which cannot be satisfied with what we call pleasure, or the mere accumulation of things. We have deeper hungers.

Atheism, I believe, is on the lips rather than in the hearts of people. Even the most worldly know moments when they cannot help thinking of their hidden origin and destiny, times when they sense that something is missing from their lives, times, when a sudden awareness overtakes them that at the back of all things is a Reality greater than themselves.

So it is with the thirst for goodness. It is doubtful if the longing for the nobler life ever completely dies. When men read the story of the Good Samaritan, they feel instinctively the pull of its truth and power. Genuine compassion has a universal and timeless appeal. It is a language we all understand.

On Christmas Eve, churches in many parts of Scotland are packed with worshippers. Some may come because it is the done thing, or because of the novelty of the hour. But I suspect that with others there is a deeper reason, something to do with the fact that deep down we sense that life is more than meat, and the body more than raiment. The thirst for God and goodness is not dead.

*　　*　　*

Too often when we consider the joys of Christmas we settle for the lesser joys.

102

Straightening up Christmas

'With the poor and mean and lowly
Lived on earth our Saviour holy.'

When we see a picture which is not hanging straight, do we in the presence of our host or hostess go and straighten it, or do we wait until they leave the room and then make the necessary adjustment, or do we leave it alone?

I heard once of a woman who had a compulsion to straighten pictures. One Christmas while visiting her neighbour, she noticed that a painting of the manger scene was slightly squint. When the neighbour left the room to make a coffee, she went over and straightened it. The moment she did so it began to play 'Still the Night'. Her confusion was considerable. The picture was deliberately designed to embarrass all who touched it. It made music only when straightened.

That story is for me a parable. Christmas having become so lop-sided, it is not surprising that the Christmas music, 'Peace on earth, goodwill to all', often gets lost in the frantic preChristmas treadmill and orgy of spending.

My concern about the lopsidedness of Christmas is shared by a charity called 'Crisis at Christmas'. For more than twenty years in a massive disused bus garage near London's Euston Station, a thousand homeless people are cared for round the clock by more than seven hundred volunteers – students, nurses, housewives, accountants, electricians, soldiers – all foregoing their own Christmas for a few hours, or a day, and some even for a week. Freda Evans who for many years was in charge says, 'We can't mend broken dreams, but for at least one week a year we can offer the homeless some decent food, decent clothes, a warm bed, companionship and a modicum of dignity.'

What a glorious attempt to straighten up Christmas, to make audible in our day the angelic chorus 'Goodwill to all', for as the carol reminds us, Jesus has a special concern for the poor, the mean and the lowly.

*   *   *

Is it True?

John Betjeman poses the question:

> And is it true and is it true
> The most tremendous tale of all,
> Seen in a stained glass window's hue
> A baby in an ox's stall.
> The maker of the stars and sea
> Became a child on earth for me.

I can understand those who refuse to accept the staggering claim made by Paul, that Jesus is 'the visible expression of the invisible God and the other claims which Jesus made for himself, that those who had seen him, now know what kind of Father God is, that he is 'the light of the world', and 'the way, the truth and the life.'

I can understand those who say he must have been out of his mind. But I have difficulty understanding those who profess to believe that 'the maker of the stars and sea, became a child on earth', but no longer marvel at the wonder of it. I would question whether anyone has the right to believe in the Incarnation who has not at first thought it incredible.

It is surely significant that the amazing claims made about Jesus were first made by those who lived closely with him for three years. The crowd may speak of someone in superlative terms, but the close friend who sees him at all hours, at night when he is tired, in the morning before he is properly awake, or when disappointment comes, or when he is off guard and under no temptation to pose, seldom thinks of his friend as a saint. It is proverbial that no one is a hero to his valet. And yet in the case of Jesus it was the disciples, those who knew him intimately, who knew him when he was tired, hungry, disappointed and hunted to death, who regarded the amazing claims he made entirely fitting. It was these same men who went out into the Roman Empire with the thrilling message that in Jesus of Nazareth, they had glimpsed the glory of God, full of grace and truth.

*   *   *

Roman Catholicism in Peru has been considerably influenced by Indian culture. Around Christmas a sign is erected on the old Cathedral in the City of Cuzco. 'Olé Jesus'. I initially thought it meant 'Holy Jesus', but in fact it means, 'Hooray for Jesus'.

Christmas Lights

A Mr Mitchell of North Carolina, tells how one Christmas he could hardly believe his eyes. He pulled his car over to the side of the road and got out to take a closer look. No, he wasn't seeing things. There were Christmas lights in a graveyard. Someone had put beautiful white lights all over the evergreen trees that surrounded the cemetery. Mr Mitchell's first reaction was that a cemetery seemed a strange place for Christmas lights, yet the more he thought about it, the more it made sense. Christmas began to take on a whole new meaning, for Jesus, by his coming into the world, had shed light into every part of its darkness, even into the darkness of death.

Having lived for most of my life in well-lit cities, I never knew how dark it could be until I came to live and minister in the Highlands. I remember going out one night to visit in Birichen, a crofting area, a few miles from Dornoch. It was so dark that nothing was visible. Suddenly out of the darkness there came a lightning flash. It lasted only a second, but in that split second the whole landscape was lit up. The hills, the Dornoch Firth, the scattered crofts all suddenly became visible. Then the darkness closed in again. I sometimes think of Jesus as that lightning flash, revealing for a short time the eternal heart of God, revealing the love that lies at the heart of the darkness and mystery of our world.

'God so loved the world that He sent his only Son.' The real wonder of Christmas is that it reminds us of the divine love from which nothing can separate us or our loved ones, that at the back of all things love reigns and God cares deeply. Dr Bill Coffin who lost his son in a drowning accident, expressed it memorably when he said, 'I am certain that when Alec died in Boston Harbour, God's was the first heart to break.'

Christmas lights in a graveyard! It makes sense.

*   *   *

To an open house in the evening
Home shall men come,
To an older place than Eden,
And a taller town than Rome.
To the end of the way of the wandering star,
To the things that cannot be and that are,
To the place where God was homeless
And all men are at home.

G K Chesterton.

We won't have a Christmas this year, you say
For now the children have all gone away;
And the house is so lonely, so quiet and so bare,
We couldn't have a Christmas that they didn't share.

We won't have a Christmas this year, you sigh,
For Christmas means things that money must buy.
Misfortune and illness have robbed us we fear
Of the things that we'd need to make Christmas this year.

We won't have a Christmas this year you weep,
For a loved one is gone, and our grief is too deep;
It will be a long time before our hearts heal,
And the spirit of Christmas again we can feel.

But if you lose Christmas when troubles befall,
You never have really had Christmas at all.
For once you have had it, it cannot depart
When you learn that true Christmas is Christ in your heart.

Verna S Teeuwissen.

A composer who was asked to write a national anthem for some distant country, declined because, as he said, 'I do not live there.' Likewise Jesus could not have composed such deathless music for our world if he had not lived among us through birth and death. The fact that he was painfully human is central to the Christian faith.

We are told that Rip Van Winkle slept for twenty years. When he finally awoke, the townspeople were so delighted they decided to hold a great Christmas feast. They said to Rip, 'Some wine?'. 'Yes thank you' was the reply. They said, 'Some Christmas pudding?' 'Yes please' said Rip. But when they finally inquired whether he would have coffee, he replied, 'Better make it decaffeinated. Regular keeps me awake.'

Frankly I am worried. Three weeks to Christmas and not a sign of an Easter egg in the shops!

Down to Earth

In the late 1940s the editorial committee of the Penguin Classic series decided that a new translation should be made of the four gospels from the Greek. Wanting an unbiased translation, E V Rieu who was a recognised agnostic as well as eminent Greek scholar, was invited to undertake the work. The story is told how a friend said to a member of Rieu's family, who was a practising Christian, 'I wonder what your father will do to the Gospels?' 'I wonder,' came the reply, 'what the Gospels will do to my father?' To translate the Gospels, E V Rieu had to study them in depth. This had a profound effect on him. In the introduction to his translation, he wrote: 'Of what I have learnt from these documents in the course of my task, I will say only this, that they bear the seal of the Son of Man and God, they are the Magna Carta of the human spirit. Were we to devote to their comprehension a little of the selfless enthusiasm that is now expended on the riddle of our physical surroundings, we should cease to say that Christianity is coming to an end – we might even feel it had only just begun.'

*   *   *

'The story of how Jesus came to earth, what he said and did here, and how he left the world while still remaining in it, has, it is safe to say, been more told, mulled over, analysed and illustrated, than any other in history. So many hands! So many versions and interpretations! We have the historical Jesus, the freedom-fighting Jesus, the proletarian Jesus. Today's revisions of Jesus' essential message claim that his kingdom is of this world, that man can live by bread alone, and must lay up treasure on earth in an ever increasing gross national product. Future historians are likely to conclude that the more we know about Jesus, the less we knew him or heeded his words.'

Malcolm Muggeridge.

'Is part of the problem of Christmas that it has not been made secular enough, sufficiently 'down to earth' to make ordinary folk see what Christ's coming means for their daily life? As I look back over my own life, I find that my own problem was not that of putting religion back into Christmas, but of putting Christmas into my religion.'

Dr Charles Duthie.

'If God ever revealed himself to man, if ever heaven appeared on earth, it was in the person and work of Jesus of Nazareth. He is beyond any shadow of doubt, and by the reluctant consent of sceptics and infidels, the wisest of the wise, the purest of the pure, and the mightiest of the mighty. His Cross has become the tree of life to all nations. His teaching is still the highest standard of religious truth. His example the unsurpassed ideal of holiness; the Gospels and Epistles of his Galilean disciples are still the book of books, more powerful than all the classics of human wisdom and genius.'

Dr Philip Schaff.

'Twas the Day After Christmas

'Twas the day after Christmas, when all through the town
Every creature was stirring, taking ornaments down.

The lights were extinguished, the candles all burned,
Empty boxes abounded wherever you turned.

The children were cranky, they'd been good for soooo long
That their innards were bursting to do something wrong.

The toys of which visions had danced in their heads
Lay abandoned in corners, their batteries dead.

When you sprang to the window and opened the sash,
Your eyes were assaulted by mountains of trash.

So it's back to the office, to the matters at hand,
As relief, like an aspirin, spreads through the land,

And the windows in outlines of colours once bright,
Now returned to dark shadows, as black as the night.

The fires of warm feelings were beginning to wane,
Like the hard, icy touch of a cold windowpane.

As the world, like the dread of an overcast day,
Reverted to form, to its patterns of grey,

When what in our wondering ears should we hear,
But the Word of the Father to be of good cheer;

To take hold of the light that will never go out,
And carry it high, and spread it about.

Throw the holly and the ivy out if you will,
But the star is before you. Follow it still.

The wonder of Christmas, of God coming here,
Cannot be confined to the end of the year,

For the light of the manger, which is now packed away,
Continues to shine and glows brighter each day,

As the people of God respond to his call
And take this, the true meaning of Christmas to all.

Ken Goodrich.

Dismantling the Tree

Well so that is that. Now we must dismantle the tree.
Putting the decorations back into their cardboard boxes –
Some have got broken   and carrying them up to the attic.
The holly and the mistletoe must be taken down and burnt,
And the children got ready for school. There are enough
Left-overs to do, warmed up, for the rest of the week –
Not that we have much appetite, having drunk such a lot,
Stayed up so late, attempted – quite unsuccessfully –
To love all our relatives, and in general
Grossly overestimated our powers. Once again
As in previous years we have seen the actual Vision and failed
To do more than entertain it as an agreeable
Possibility, once again we have sent Him away,
Begging though to remain His disobedient servant.

(Extract from the poem 'For the Time Being' by W H Auden)

Christmas Extravagance

(Twelve Suggestions for Christmas)

1. Treat strangers and friends to an abundance of goodwill.

2. Give away many smiles and words of kindness.

3. Give thanks again and again.

4. Give soft answers and mend quarrels.

5. Listen, laugh and encourage more.

6. Take greater delight in the beauty and wonder of the earth.

7. Do good turns to people in need without being found out.

8. Give generously to the poor and starving.

9. Give your presence to the lonely.

10. At home speak your love each day.

11. Make time for worship.

12. Light many candles and give them to the Darkness.